Freelance from the Flight Deck

By
Joshua P. Vinson

Table of Contents

Introduction: Welcome to the World of Corporate Contract Flying..4

Chapter 1: Understanding the Contract Pilot Lifestyle 13

Chapter 2: Qualifications, Legal Setup, and Recurrent Training .28

Chapter 3: Finding Work and Building Your Network.................39

Chapter 4: Setting Your Rates and Negotiating Contracts............52

Chapter 5: Mastering the Corporate Aviation Experience............62

Chapter 6: Managing Your Schedule and Work-Life Balance......73

Chapter 7: Financial Planning for Contract Pilots........................86

Chapter 8: Long-Term Success & Expanding Your Opportunities 98

Conclusion: Your Next Steps to Becoming a Successful Contract Pilot 108

About the Author 112

Welcome to the World of Corporate Contract Flying

The Rise of the Contract Pilot

Once upon a time, the path to professional aviation success was clear and unwavering. You went to flight school, built time at a regional airline, climbed the seniority ladder, and eventually retired with a commemorative plaque, a gold-striped hat, and a pension that might keep up with inflation. But somewhere along the way, things began to shift. Pilots started looking around and wondering: Is this really the only way to fly for a living? More importantly, does it have to be this rigid, this structured, this ... grounded in someone else's idea of success? Enter the contract pilot: a breed of aviator who values flexibility, independence, and the ability to call the shots. The rise of the contract pilot has gained popularity with the increase of gig economy workers. And you, dear reader, are here at just the right time.

I'll shine some light on the more obscure career option in professional aviation: contract flying. This is not a tell-all or memoir but a guide that I hope will bring you through everything necessary to become a successful contract pilot. There are plenty of resources and writings for pilots going from zero to hero with an airline or even corporate flying. But there's little to be found in regard to becoming a successful contract pilot, and with this book, I intend to fill that gap.

I never set out to be a contract pilot. In fact, I had visions of myself wearing the crisp airline uniform, sipping mediocre airport coffee, and collecting a predictable paycheck while complaining about crew scheduling. But after several years, I realized that the structured world of airline flying wasn't for me. I wanted freedom. I wanted adventure. And most importantly, I wanted to be my own boss and have control of my time. So, I ditched the seniority list and jumped headfirst into the unpredictable, thrilling, and sometimes mildly terrifying world of corporate contract flying. This book will expose concepts and ideas that will help you become more successful as a contract pilot and guide your transition into self-employment. Along the way, we will cover some of the issues that will arise as a freelance pilot, as well as the perks. We're going to walk through how to find high-paying gigs, how to build a thriving freelance business, and, just as importantly, how to balance the intoxicating freedom of freelancing with the ever-practical need for steady income and long-term career growth.

The Shift from a Structured Career Path to Freelancing

If there's a poster child for structured aviation careers, it's the airline pilot. Unionized, seniority-based, and meticulously scheduled, it's a world that thrives on routine and predictability. For decades, it made perfect sense. Airline pilots earned solid wages, had clear career progression, and enjoyed benefits like retirement plans and travel perks. But cracks started forming in that model, especially after the 2008 financial crisis and the more recent pandemic disruptions.

Pilots began to realize that airline careers came with trade-offs: years spent commuting, rigid schedules, and a lifestyle that often meant missing birthdays, holidays, and family dinners. Add to that mergers, furloughs, and ever-changing company policies, and suddenly, the dream job felt more like golden handcuffs.

In contrast, the contract flying lifestyle offered something airlines never could: freedom. The freedom to choose which days you work. The freedom to negotiate your rate. The freedom to fly for operators you respect (and walk away from the ones you don't). Instead of climbing a seniority list, contract pilots build a reputation. And instead of waiting ten years to upgrade, they take the jobs they're qualified for and get paid accordingly.

This shift from airline loyalty to freelance entrepreneurship is a mindset change. It's not for everyone, but it's gaining momentum. Pilots are recognizing that they can have a career that's flexible, lucrative, and enjoyable. Many are keeping their airline positions but flying contract gigs on days off. Others are going all-in on freelancing. Either way, the message is clear: professional pilots want options. And the contract path gives them more than they've ever had before.

Why Corporate Aviation Is Booming

To understand the rise of the contract pilot, you first have to understand the explosion happening in corporate aviation. What was once reserved for the ultra-wealthy and Fortune 500 execs, private flying has become increasingly accessible and necessary for businesses and individuals who want to avoid the hassles, delays, and unpredictability of commercial airlines. The COVID-19 pandemic accelerated this shift, as health concerns and flight cancellations pushed people toward private travel. Suddenly, jet cards, fractional ownership, and on-demand charters weren't just luxury conveniences; they were practical solutions.

This boom didn't slow down once the pandemic dust settled. In fact, it gained momentum. Remote work became the norm, and companies realized they could operate without being tied to a single location; as a result, business travel rebounded with a vengeance. Wealth creation continued in the tech, finance, and startup sectors, and with it came an increase in private jet users. These aren't just billionaires flying once a year; they're entrepreneurs, investors, families, and executives flying often and expecting a higher level of service.

Corporate aviation grew to meet the demand, but flight departments and operators quickly found themselves facing a talent shortage. Full-time pilots were in short supply, and many were unwilling to give up the predictability and perks of their airline or government jobs. The solution? Freelancers. Highly qualified, reliable, adaptable pilots who could step into the left or right seat on short notice, handle the job professionally, and move on to the next opportunity. As the industry expanded, so did the need for skilled contract pilots, and what was once a niche became an essential part of the aviation ecosystem.

Is Contract Flying Right for You?

By now, you might be thinking, "This all sounds great, but is it really for me?" Every aspiring contract pilot must ask themselves this question. Because while this lifestyle offers freedom, flexibility, and financial upside, it also demands adaptability, business sense, and the ability to thrive in uncertainty. Contract flying isn't just a career; it's a small business. You are the brand, the talent, and the product. You're the pilot, the scheduler, the accountant, the marketing department, and the customer service rep. That can be intimidating, but it's also incredibly empowering. You set your own course. You build your own network. You create your own opportunities.

Do you enjoy variety? One month, you could be flying a family to the Caribbean. Next, you might be covering a corporate shuttle between New York and Chicago. No two jobs are the same, and no two operators work exactly alike. If you thrive in dynamic environments and like meeting new people, contract flying might be your perfect match.

Are you self-motivated? Nobody's going to remind you to keep your recurrent training up to date or send that invoice on time. Success in this field depends on how seriously you approach the business side of flying. If you're proactive, organized, and willing to hustle a little, the rewards are worth it.

Do you value autonomy? Some pilots love the camaraderie of a full-time crew, the comfort of a consistent base, and the rhythm of scheduled flying. Others would rather pick and choose their clients, aircraft, and travel days. If you're the kind of person who prefers setting your own rules, contract flying is about as self-directed as it gets.

Ultimately, only you can decide whether this path is right for you. But if you're looking for a flying career that offers variety, independence, and unlimited potential, then you're in the right place. This book is your guide to navigating that world. From setting your rates and finding work to staying healthy on the road and building a brand that gets you steady work, everything you need is here.

What Is Corporate Contract Flying?

Corporate contract flying is the freelance version of being a professional pilot. Instead of working for a single airline or company, contract pilots offer their services on an as-needed basis to corporate flight departments, private jet owners, and charter operators. Think of it like being a highly skilled mercenary—except instead of fighting battles, you're flying multi-million-dollar jets for executives, business owners, and people who have way too much money to deal with airport security lines. Some pilots contract on a part-time basis to supplement their primary job, while others go full-time and make an entire career out of it. I am the latter. You might fly a Gulfstream one week, a Citation the next, and then find yourself in a King Air, wondering if you should have asked more questions before accepting the gig. I can guarantee you this: it's never boring.

Why More Pilots Are Choosing Freelance Over Traditional Airline Careers

Pilots are creatures of habit, but we also love a good escape plan. The traditional airline career path begins at the regionals, where you claw your way up the seniority list, bid for better schedules, and pray your airline doesn't merge or furlough you. Then, you start this process all over again at a major or legacy carrier. For obvious reasons, it's not as appealing as it once was. Contract flying is a great escape hatch for pilots who want more control over their lives.

The biggest reason pilots are choosing freelance work? Freedom. Instead of being locked into a rigid airline schedule, contract pilots decide when and where they want to work. No more missing birthdays, holidays, or anniversaries unless you actually want to (which might be the case for some). If you want to take three weeks off to backpack through Europe or finally finish that home improvement project you started five years ago, you can. Or, as it was in my case, I needed more flexibility in my relationship with aviation. I wanted to take off work when I wanted to and not when the vacation bid award said I could. Also, I wanted to be able to work more if I needed to or wanted to.

Then there's the money. Contract pilots can earn significantly more per day than their airline counterparts, especially if they specialize in high-demand aircraft. While airline pilots are bound to union pay scales, contract pilots set their own rates and negotiate directly with clients. If you play your cards right, you can work fewer days and make the same, if not more, than you would in some traditional airline jobs. Of course, not everything is sunshine and upgraded hotel rooms. Contract flying comes with its share of uncertainty. Unlike airline pilots, who have that guaranteed paycheck, contract pilots only get paid when they fly. There's no sick leave, no health benefits, and no pension plan waiting at the end of your career. If you're the type of person who breaks out in hives at the thought of financial unpredictability, this might not be your dream job.

Being a contract pilot is a bit like dating. Some gigs are incredible. You get treated well, paid on time, and they want to see you again. Others leave you stranded in the middle of nowhere, wondering why you ever agreed to this in the first place. In time, you will weed out the clients that are not suitable for you. Despite the challenges, most contract pilots wouldn't trade this lifestyle for anything. The freedom, variety, and financial potential make it one of the most exciting and rewarding career paths in the aviation industry.

Who This Book Is For and What You'll Learn

If you're reading this book, chances are you're at least a little intrigued by the idea of corporate contract flying. Maybe you're an airline pilot looking for a side hustle, a charter pilot ready to take the leap into full-time freelancing, or a flight instructor wondering if there's more out there than teaching steep turns to student pilots. Whatever your background, I hope this book will give you the tools, knowledge, and ideas to build a successful career as a contract pilot.

Stepping into the freelance world of aviation is exciting, but it's also full of nuances you don't always learn in flight school. That's where this book comes in. It's your guide to locating opportunities

11

and turning a profit in the world of corporate contract flying. You'll find not just tips and tricks but a full blueprint for launching, growing, and sustaining your career as a contract pilot.

This book isn't just a collection of advice; it's a practical, actionable blueprint for building a sustainable freelance aviation career. If you follow the step-by-step approach and employ the concepts discussed here, you won't just dream about becoming a successful contract pilot; you'll actually become one.

We'll cover everything from how to get started and find work to setting your rates and negotiating contracts. You'll learn the secrets of networking, how to avoid common pitfalls, and strategies for keeping clients coming back for more. By the end, you'll have a clear roadmap for building a thriving career as a contractor in corporate aviation—one that puts you in control of your schedule, your income, and your future. And along the way, I promise to keep it real. No sugarcoating, no unrealistic promises—just honest advice from someone who's been there, made the mistakes, and lived to tell the tale. So buckle up because this is going to be an adventure. Welcome to the world of corporate contract flying, where no two days are the same, and the sky is quite literally the limit.

CHAPTER 1

Understanding the
Contract Pilot Lifestyle

What Is a Corporate Contract Pilot?

I use the terms "corporate contract pilot," "contract pilot," and "contractor" synonymously throughout this book. Corporate contract pilot is the most comprehensive descriptor, but it's also a mouthful. Most of the contract flying done around the country is tied to an organization, hence the corporate part. "Corporate contract pilot" is a term I have strung together. We're the aviation industry's equivalent of highly skilled hired guns. We swoop in when needed, handle business with expert precision, get paid well for our time, and then disappear into the horizon until the next call comes in. We're independent, adaptable, and able to slip into a new cockpit and make it seem like we've been flying that plane for years. It's an exciting, challenging, and sometimes ridiculous way to make a living. But for those of us who crave freedom, variety, and control over our schedules, it's the dream job. Make no mistake, this is a lifestyle business. You'll have to be a highly active part of the operation in the beginning until you are able to scale your business (which we will cover in a later chapter). Oftentimes, you will become an integral part of other people's businesses and lives as you build your client base. These clients may become friends, colleagues, and, in some cases, future partners. But I am getting ahead of myself. For now, just know that corporate contract pilots are not spending years crawling up a seniority list while flying the same three routes over and over again like an airline pilot. They are not W-2 corporate pilot guys with a set salary, guaranteed days off, and vacation time. Contract pilots are the hustlers of aviation.

The Differences Between Contract, Charter, and Airline Flying

Before diving headfirst into the world of contract flying, let's get something straight: Not all flying jobs are created equal. If you're new to the corporate world of aviation or still straddling different aviation paths, it's worth understanding how contract flying stacks up against airline and charter flying. Some pilots use pay, equipment, and quality of life as their gauges to assess aviation opportunities. Let's touch on the four main options for flying as a professional pilot in the civilian world.

Airline Pilots: The 9-to-5 of the Skies (Without the 9-to-5 Hours)

Airline pilots enjoy structured schedules, consistent pay, and a seniority system that ensures they gradually move up the ranks unless their airline merges, furloughs, or suddenly goes bankrupt. They fly the same routes week after week, operating within a tightly controlled system. The predictability can be comforting, but for those who crave variety and autonomy, it can feel like Groundhog Day at 35,000 feet.

The perks? Airline pilots get union protection, retirement benefits, and a steady paycheck. The downsides? They trade flexibility for stability, and many spend years paying their dues in the right seat before upgrading to captain. Plus, if you hate the idea of spending a substantial amount of time in busy airport terminals and dealing with TSA every day, a traditional airline pilot may not be the gig for you. If you don't like the idea of being in the commercial airports around the masses day in and day out, you may want to reconsider. I couldn't wait in long lines to use the bathroom or get coffee and food every day, all while the 3-1-1 carry-on rule was blasted on repeat over the PA system. The incessant "If you see something, say something" message over the speaker made me say something, all right. I said, "I'm outta here the first chance I get!" But in all fairness, some people have the capacity and the personality for this type of work environment, and that is fantastic. We need airline pilots, but I am here to discuss contract flying and shine some light on the benefits of this lesser-known option of aviation employment.

Charter Pilots and Corporate Pilots: The Middle Ground Between Structure and Spontaneity

Charter flying, regulated under Part 135 of the Federal Aviation Regulations (FAR), provides a bit more variety than the airlines. Charter pilots fly on demand, meaning schedules can be unpredictable, but they still work for a company that employs them full-time. You are probably wearing a uniform and may be punching a clock. You will be flying with other people in the company for crewed trips. There is usually a way to move up within the company. You may start out on a smaller airframe and move up to a larger one. These companies operate private jets for businesses and high-net-worth individuals who prefer the convenience of flying on their own terms. Sometimes, the aircraft are owned by the charter company, and in some cases, they are leased or owned by the clients.

Charter pilots get a mix of stability and adventure. They work with VIP passengers, fly to interesting destinations, and sometimes get the privilege of last-minute schedule changes. They typically earn less than corporate pilots and airline pilots, but this is always changing. I have seen some individuals earn a very good living as charter pilots. There was a time when NetJets was one of the best charter jobs around.

Corporate Pilot (Not Contract)

Most corporate flying is done under FAR Part 91. This provides a certain amount of flexibility. Think of places like AT&T, Coca-Cola, Cox Communications, or Lowes. They have their own flight department within the organization. Their aircraft are usually all the same type. The flight department has a hierarchy with a director of operations, a chief pilot, in-house maintenance, and other subcommittees and subordinates. As a pilot, you are given a compensation package (usually negotiable at hire), and you share the flying with other pilots in the flight department. Depending on the company, this can be a sweet gig. Even better if it's a good schedule and decent equipment. In some cases, your compensation can consist of company stock and other fringe benefits that you would not receive at an airline or charter job. This may include a free phone, a company car, or the option to keep your personal plane in the company hangar. You may also get to keep a job with the company if you've lost your medical.

Freight Dogs

We can't skip over the freight dogs, or we may never get another Amazon package! UPS, FedEx, and Amazon all run operations similar to airlines. Most of the flying is done at night, and the pay is very competitive. The corporate structure is typical of an airline, featuring a standard hierarchy, chain of command, and seniority list for pilots. Schedules and routes are usually set ahead of time, so you will know when you are expected to fly. The equipment can vary widely, ranging from single-engine turbo-props to large aircraft such as MD-11s and Boeing 767s.

Corporate Contract Pilots: The Freelancers of the Aviation World

Contract pilots take on freelance flying gigs for flight departments, private owners, and charter companies that need temporary crew members. They might fill in for a sick pilot, help during busy seasons, or provide expertise for a specific aircraft type. Most contract flying is done under FAR Part 91. Unlike charter pilots, they're not tied to a single employer, and unlike airline pilots, they don't have to wait years to move up the ranks. The trade-off? No guaranteed income. If you're not flying, you're not getting paid.

But the benefits? Complete control over your schedule, potentially higher daily pay, and the thrill of not knowing where you'll be flying next week. One week, you might be flying a Fortune 500 executive to a board meeting in New York, and the next, you could be ferrying a family on their island vacation in the Bahamas. It's never boring, and for those who thrive in a dynamic environment, it's the perfect fit.

17

The Key Players in Corporate Aviation: Who's Hiring Contract Pilots?

If you're considering contract flying, it helps to know where the jobs come from. Unlike airlines, which have a centralized hiring process, the corporate aviation world is more fragmented. Here are the key players you'll be working with:

Flight Departments: The Private Jet HQs

Large corporations, wealthy individuals, and private investment firms often have in-house flight departments that manage their aircraft. These flight departments hire full-time pilots but often need contract pilots to fill gaps in their schedules. Some departments operate just one or two aircraft, while others have an entire fleet of jets at their disposal. When one or more of their pilots are out for sickness, vacation, or training, they could be shorthanded. Getting in with a flight department is one of the best ways to secure consistent contract work. Once you've flown for them and proven yourself reliable, they'll call you back whenever they need an extra set of hands.

Aircraft Owners and Operators

A large number of aircraft owners use contract pilots to operate their missions. You become their "guy" for running their trips. The owners will contact you directly to coordinate their trip needs. You may be asked to keep an eye on things with the airplane. You could be responsible for general upkeep and stocking in addition to flying the aircraft.

Then you have owners who operate their own aircraft, too. This provides some work opportunities as well. Whether the trip logistics call for repositioning the aircraft or a second set of eyes for the flight, there are opportunities in knowing aircraft owners. Some insurance companies require owner-operators to fly with a pro pilot (you) until the owner has accumulated a certain amount of time in type. This can be a great short-term contract gig.

Aircraft Managers

Some private jet owners don't want to deal with flight departments or operators, so they hire aircraft managers to handle the logistics. These managers oversee scheduling, maintenance, and pilot staffing on behalf of the owner. Aircraft managers can gatekeep a lot of contract work! If you can develop a relationship with an aircraft manager, you could end up being their go-to contract pilot whenever the owner(s) need to fly. This is a wonderful way to stay busy with work and grow your network, which we will cover in a bit. The challenge? These jobs are often based on personal connections rather than formal job postings. If you want to get on an aircraft manager's radar, you need to network like your career depends on it—because, well, it does.

Common Aircraft Flown in Corporate Aviation

The aircraft you fly as a contract pilot will depend on your experience and type ratings. Some aircraft are more common than others, and having the right qualifications can open doors to higher-paying gigs.

Light Jets (The Starters):

Cessna Citation CJ series

Embraer Phenom 100/300

HondaJet

Midsize Jets (The Workhorses):

Hawker 800XP

Cessna Citation XLS

Embraer Legacy 450

Super-Midsize Jets (The Sweet Spot):

Gulfstream G280

Bombardier Challenger 350

Dassault Falcon 2000

Large Cabin and Ultra-Long-Range Jets (The Dream Machines):

Gulfstream G650/G700

Bombardier Global 7500

Dassault Falcon 8X

If you're looking to maximize your earnings as a contract pilot, specializing in high-demand aircraft types is a good way to go. Obtain a type rating of a common plane in your area, and you'll find yourself in high demand. Though, you can totally contract in aircraft that do not require type ratings. There is a lot of contract work in TBMs, King Airs, and even Cirrus, to name a few.

The Pros and Cons of Contract Flying

With full-time W-2 employment, pilots only need to consider the pay, the equipment they are flying, and their quality of life to get a good idea of how the job will serve them. With contract flying, we need to dive a little deeper to determine the pros and cons.

Flexibility and Earning Potential

One of the biggest reasons pilots opt for contract flying is the flexibility and freedom. Unlike airline pilots who are at the mercy of seniority lists and scheduled blocks, contract pilots choose when and where they want to work. Want to take a month off to pursue other interests? No problem. Need to work nonstop for a couple of months to pay cash for an upcoming expense? You can do that, too. It's all about personal choice and having free agency to work accordingly. Then there's the earning potential. On a per-day basis, contract pilots often make more than their full-time counterparts. A seasoned contract pilot flying a high-demand jet aircraft can make $1,200 to $2,500 a day (2025 numbers, location dependent, and your mileage may vary). It may be even more for international or last-minute gigs. The downside? If you're not flying, you're not earning. There are no sick days, paid vacations, or guaranteed income streams. You could be flush with cash one month and scrambling for work the next, so financial planning is key.

Unpredictable Schedules

While flexibility is fantastic, unpredictability is the flip side. One week, you're turning down trips because you're too busy; the next, your phone is eerily silent. You have to be comfortable with feast-or-famine cycles in the beginning. I will show how to mitigate this in a later chapter. Contract pilots live and die by their reputations and ability to network. Your last flight could be just that if you develop a reputation for being unreliable or difficult to work with. The phone will stop ringing quickly. There are a fair amount of last-minute trip requests that you will need to be able to manage as part of the job, too. It's not as difficult as it sounds, but expect it once you begin to build a client base. It's a judgment call each time on a short-notice trip request, and you live with your decisions. The flexibility is great, but if you're someone who needs a structured schedule and guaranteed days off, contract flying might give you an ulcer.

Managing Finances and Benefits as a Freelancer

Here's where things get tricky. As a contract pilot, you are your own boss, which also means the accounting and financial planning is on you, too. There's no company direct deposit coming in bi-weekly and certainly no pension waiting for you at the end of your career. Everything is on you. Managing finances wisely is going to be crucial. We will discuss this more in a later chapter, but know upfront that managing irregular income is part of the game.

Health insurance is another challenge. Without an employer-sponsored plan, contract pilots must find private coverage or join a professional association that offers group plans.

Despite the financial and logistical challenges, many contract pilots wouldn't trade this lifestyle for anything. The ability to control your career, maximize earnings, and avoid the bureaucratic headaches of traditional aviation jobs makes it all worthwhile. If you can handle the uncertainty and plan ahead financially, contract flying can be one of the most rewarding paths in aviation.

Which Is Right for You?

So, you've got a decent amount of flight time, and now you're standing at the crossroads of aviation career choices: contract flying, corporate flying, airline flying, or freight flying? Do you go for the structured world of commercial airlines with its predictable schedules and union perks, or do you embrace the private jet life— rubbing elbows with CEOs, possible celebrities, and high net-worth individuals? Let's look at it in a way that gets to the core of the decision: your ability to earn, grow, and build your career, and what it's really like running your own aviation business.

Do You Want Freedom or Predictability?

I once had an airline pilot friend tell me, "I always know when my next day off is." As a contract pilot, I had to laugh because I never knew when my next day off was. In a nutshell, that's the scheduling difference between airline and corporate flying and contract flying. Another stark difference is being asked to fly (as a contract pilot) versus being told to fly (as an employee). This may not be a concern to some, but as a contract pilot, you are asked to fly, and that's nice.

Airline pilots operate on a strict schedule. Seniority dictates most everything: when you fly, what you fly, where you fly, and what holidays you'll miss. If you're new to an airline, expect to work weekends, holidays, and red-eye flights before you get the "good" routes. But once you climb the seniority ladder, things get better. Long-haul pilots, for example, may only work a few trips per month and have plenty of downtime in between. One of the biggest perks is that when an airline pilot is off-duty, they are truly off-duty. No middle-of-the-night phone calls, no last-minute schedule changes, no "Hey, can you take this trip tomorrow?" messages from a flight department manager.

Contract pilots don't have a union-backed schedule. One week, you might be sipping coffee at home for days with no flights, and the next, you're on a whirlwind five-day trip across the country. Some corporate operators have scheduled flying, but many are on-demand, meaning you need to be available when the client needs to travel. A client can decide at the last minute that they want to go somewhere, and guess what? You're the lucky pilot making that happen. The upside is flexibility and control. If you build a strong network as a contract pilot or work for a company that respects downtime, you can carve out a work-life balance that suits you. The downside is the balance isn't always guaranteed.

Pay Structures and Job Stability: The Big Trade-Off

Let's talk about money. At the end of the day, passion for aviation is great, but passion doesn't pay the bills or buy that retirement home you've been dreaming about.

Airline pilots operate on a seniority-based pay scale. A first-year regional airline first officer might make $50,000–$80,000, while a seasoned captain at a major airline can rake in more than $350,000 per year (2025 numbers). The catch is it takes years to reach that level. Pilots who join airlines later in life often find themselves stuck playing catch-up on the seniority list.

But here's the kicker: stability. Airlines rarely lay off pilots unless there's a massive industry shake-up (pandemics, bankruptcies, or mergers). Once you're in, you're in. You get retirement benefits, health insurance, and a solid paycheck even if you fly a light schedule. It's a career path built on longevity and, dare I say, security.

A full-time corporate pilot can make anywhere from $90,000 to over $250,000 per year, with additional company benefits. In some cases, the additional bonuses and stock options are offered.

Contract pilots, on the other hand, can command $1,000–$2,500 per day on most corporate jets, but they don't get paid when they're not flying. Contract pilots lack the stability airline pilots enjoy. Corporate flight departments can close overnight. Owners can sell jets at the drop of a hat. One day, you're the trusted captain of a Falcon 7X, and the next, the company decides to downgrade to a Phenom 300 (which they already have a pilot for). This type of work can be far more radical than the airlines, but often more lucrative in the short term.

Client Expectations and Service Standards between Airline and Corporate

Airline passengers have pretty low expectations. As long as you get them from A to B safely (and preferably on time), they are not too concerned. No one's asking you to book them a rental car or if there is coffee and ice on board before takeoff. In fact, most passengers forget you exist unless there's turbulence or a delay.

Your job is to fly the plane. Sure, you have to deal with the occasional grumpy traveler or the person who tries to act entitled, but in general, airline pilots have zero interaction with passengers beyond an automated welcome message and an ETA update over the PA.

Corporate flying is a whole different ball game. You're not just the pilot. You're part of the experience. Your passengers expect a certain level of service, and that means ensuring everything is clean, stocked, and ready to go. They want a smooth ride that's on their schedule, stocked with their favorite snacks and drinks. In corporate flying, the details matter. But here's the flip side: if you deliver excellent service, they remember. Corporate contract pilots who go above and beyond often find themselves rewarded with loyalty, generous tips, and long-term relationships that lead to continual work opportunities.

Conclusion

Being a corporate contract pilot isn't for everyone, but for those who thrive on variety, independence, and adventure, it's one of the best careers in aviation. You won't have the predictability of an airline schedule, but you'll have something even better: freedom. Whether you're flying CEOs, celebrities, or high net-worth individuals, one thing is certain: no two days are ever the same. And in the world of aviation, that's a pretty great way to make a living. Understanding the differences between airline and corporate contract flying is key to making an informed career choice. Contract pilots enjoy flexibility and a high earning potential, but they must navigate the complexities of networking, business management, and aircraft specialization. By building relationships with flight departments, owner-operators, and aircraft managers and obtaining type ratings in high-demand aircraft, contract pilots can create a thriving career in corporate aviation. In the next chapter, we'll explore how to get started as a contract pilot, including the qualifications, training, and legal considerations necessary for success.

CHAPTER 2

Qualifications, Legal Setup, and Recurrent Training

What You Need to Get Started

So, you've decided to dive into the world of corporate contract flying. Excellent choice! You're about to embark on a career where your office is at 40,000 feet, your schedule is your own (sort of), and your income is as limitless as your hustle. But before you start daydreaming about sipping piña coladas on a layover in an exotic destination, let's talk about some of the not-so-glamorous parts of what's required to get started on the right foot.

Requirements and Insurance Background Checks

Corporate contract pilots need at least a Second-Class Medical Certificate, though some operators will require you to hold a First-Class Medical Certificate.

Obtaining one is a straightforward process. You'll need to find an Aviation Medical Examiner (AME). They're the gatekeepers of whether you get to keep flying or if you should start exploring a career in accounting. Be honest, but don't overshare. If they ask, "Do you ever feel stressed?" don't delve into your latest existential, post-break-up crisis. Pass the physical consisting of vision, hearing, and general health checks. For most healthy pilots, this is a non-issue. However, if you have any past medical conditions, be prepared for extra paperwork, additional tests, and an infinite loop of FAA bureaucracy.

After you get your medical certificate squared away, you will need a minimum of a Commercial Pilots license to be able to charge for your services. Depending on what you are planning to fly, plan to obtain either multi-engine or single engine privileges. Insurance companies in the corporate aviation world call the shots. They ultimately have the final say about you crewing an aircraft under their coverage. Expect to complete a pilot history form with questions about your background before you start flying for clients and operators. This is produced by the insurance companies which cover the aircraft and the pilots. Plan to ask the insurance company directly what the minimum time requirements are for pilot-in-command (PIC) and/or second-in-command (SIC). Knowing this may save you some time. Additionally, if you plan to fly internationally, an up-to-date passport as well as TSA PreCheck and Global Entry are highly recommended. You will be going for speed and ease of use as you commute through airports as a passenger. Anything that gets you to work easier or, more importantly, home more quickly is worth the investment.

Minimum Flight Hours and Experience: Paying Your Dues

If the corporate aviation industry had a bouncer, lack of flight hours would have gotten you kicked out before you even reached the velvet ropes. The reality is that most corporate operators and insurance companies want to see the above mentioned credentials and at least 1,500 total hours before they consider you for acting as PIC of a jet. Some high-end operations require more hours and time in type. If you are not there, I would challenge you to figure out an agreeable way to get to that level of experience to really get your business off the ground. Ideally, you want to do this with synergy. Establish connections in the industry while building your reputation and increasing your flight time. Enjoy the process, and learn all you can. So, if you don't have 1,500-plus hours of flight time, does that mean you can't become a contract pilot? Of course not! But you are going to have a more challenging time getting insured for single-pilot operations and/or PIC qualifications.

If you've been flying as a flight instructor, you're on the right track, but you may need some turbine time before running with the big dogs. Look for right-seat opportunities to swing gear and work radios for someone in your network of airports. You may have to knock on some hangars here and there, beat the bushes, and not be too choosy. Alternatively, maybe you've been grinding it out in the regionals and are looking for a career shift. In that case, congratulations! You're already ahead of many newcomers since you have some turbine time and likely a high total time. You will need to orient yourself with how business aviation works, but at least you are likely eligible and insurable. For those lacking turbine or jet experience, getting a right-seat gig in a corporate flight department or charter operation is the best way to gain traction. Many operators will take a lower-time SIC with strong fundamentals, a great attitude, and a willingness to learn. Once you rack up some turbine time and become a solid resource, the real opportunities will start to come.

Type Ratings and Recurrent Training

One of the first questions you'll be asked when looking for contract work is, "What type ratings do you have?" For the uninitiated, simply put, a type rating is an FAA requirement for aircraft over 12,500 lbs. or turbine-powered. Some pilots self-fund their first type rating, hoping it will open doors for them. I would advise against this. You should be able to work some or all of the cost of this into your agreements in the beginning since you will likely be starting out on a smaller, more cost-efficient jet. Think of the "starters" and "workhorses" from Chapter 1. Those type ratings are a lot less costly than Challengers and Gulfstreams. Some operators and owners will pay for your type rating. Or, in most cases, a training slot is included in their purchase of the aircraft. There may be an agreement that would protect the payer (your client) from losing you as a pilot after they typed you. You may be asked to sign a training commitment or agreement when someone else pays for your type rating. This is not the end of the world, but I would not commit to much more than one year of service.

Pro tip: If you're looking for the best bang for your buck, get a type rating or gain experience in a low-cost, high-demand aircraft like the Cessna Citation, Beechjet, or Phenom. Even the King Air would work. These aircraft have large fleets, meaning more job opportunities. Additionally, knowledge of local, understaffed airplanes could be another beneficial angle to hustle up a type rating or experience.

Once you have a type rating and/or experience, don't get too comfortable because you'll need to keep it current. This means recurrent training every twelve months to keep the insurance company happy. Some training facilities are better than others when it comes to recurrent training. I've done them all: in-aircraft training, simulator training, and FAA checkrides. They all have the same layout. They start with your airwork and VFR maneuvers, followed by IFR approaches, and finish with abnormalities and emergencies. Don't get too hung up on where you do your training. Just try to get the most out of it, and make sure the training is approved by the client's insurance policy. Training facilities are also great places to network and meet other contractors.

Setting Up Your Business

If you thought gaining flight experience was the hardest part of becoming a contract pilot, I have bad news for you. Welcome to the world of self-employment. We could write multiple books on the legal structure, tax implications, tax liability, and strategies to mitigate, but I will attempt to keep this germane to what you will need to get started and get through your first few years of business.

LLC vs. Sole Proprietorship: Which Is Best?

So, do you go the sole proprietorship route, or do you set up an LLC? That depends on how much you enjoy sleeping at night. A sole proprietorship is the simplest way to operate because there is not a lot of paperwork or legal fees, just you and your pilot license. The problem with this is if something goes wrong (like, say, a client tries to sue you for something unexpected), your personal assets are on the line. If you are bootstrapping into this and just trying to get some paychecks coming in, operating as a sole proprietorship is fine for a little while. But I would not let this structure be permanent.

On the other hand, a limited liability company (LLC) creates a legal separation between you and your business. It offers some protection in case someone gets litigious. Yes, there's some paperwork and an annual fee involved, but if you're serious about contract flying, it's worth the peace of mind. You will be better off in the long run the sooner you start your LLC. In a later chapter, you'll gain an understanding of some of the accounting and tax implications that will go along with owning an LLC. For now, think about what you want your business name to be and who you can find to help you set this up!

Liability and Insurance Considerations

Most operators' insurance policies will cover liability while you're on the job, but if you freelance for multiple clients, you should consider non-owned aircraft insurance. This insurance covers liability in the event of an incident involving a rented or borrowed aircraft. The Aircraft Owners and Pilots Association (AOPA) is a good resource for this. This protects you in case something goes wrong while flying someone else's aircraft. You may also get professional liability insurance, which protects pilots from legal claims related to flight operations. Additionally, you want to be listed on the operators insurance or meet the requirements of their "open pilot" portion of their policy. This will provide you with additional coverage. The latter is the most common when contracting.

Health Insurance Options for Contract Pilots

You are mainly looking for three types of insurance here as a baseline: health insurance, some sort of disability insurance, and life

33

insurance (if someone depends on you for income). You'll want to shop around for these coverages.

For health insurance, some pilots join professional associations, such as the NBAA, to access group health plans at a lower cost. Another option would be to join your spouse's plan. Or, if you are in the United States, look at the Healthcare Marketplace.

Next is disability insurance. There are a lot of products, including short-term and long-term disability insurance. The "loss of license" (loss of medical) offered by Harvey Watt for a set amount of time is a pretty reasonable approach in my opinion. You can define the benefits to suit your needs. This would be in the event you could not obtain your medical certificate for disqualifying reasons and would serve as a form of long-term disability.

Lastly, there's life insurance. If someone depends on you for their livelihood then you will want to carry some form of life insurance. It's your call if you prefer "term" or "whole life," but either way, let's make sure your loved ones are cared for.

Managing Finances and Taxes

If tax season makes you break out in a cold sweat, you're not alone. As a contract pilot, you'll need to track your expenses, save for taxes, and claim deductions like your life depends on it—because it kind of does.

You are going to start by opening yourself a business checking account with the legal documents and the EIN you received when you established your business. Next, you will want some accounting software like QuickBooks or Quicken to help manage income and expenses. These products also offer invoice creation and billing options, which is nice. Next, you will want to locate a tax professional familiar with aviation-related business expenses so that they can help you optimize your finances and reduce your tax liability.

Since you will be staying in lots of hotels and booking numerous airline flights, you may also consider (with caution) using a business credit card for the brand of airline you travel on most and/or the hotel brand you plan to use most often. These business credit cards can also help you with categorizing expenses throughout the year and keep your personal expenses separate from your business expenses. Plus, obtaining status with a hotel or airline can make your life on the road easier, earning perks such as early check-ins, late check-outs, and priority boarding. In many cases, the credit card can help you obtain that status more quickly (please don't tell Dave Ramsey I said this!).

It is also up to you to set up and fund your retirement accounts. Corporate contract pilots cannot count on company stock options, pensions, or a matched 401(k). You have to do this yourself, and we will cover this in more detail in Chapter 7.

Certifications and Continuing Education

It's often said that a good pilot is always learning. In the world of contract flying, that mindset isn't optional; it's essential. Certification and continuing education keep you current, competitive, and confident in the cockpit. From maintaining your IFR currency to your recurrent type rating training, every hour spent learning pays off in professionalism. FAA compliance, new avionics systems, international ops, and evolving best practices are all part of the job. The most successful contract pilots don't just check the box, they seek out opportunities to grow.

Staying Compliant with FAA Regulations

The FAA regulations. If you ever find yourself struggling to sleep on an overnight, just pull up the FAR/AIM and do a little light reading. It works better than melatonin. In all seriousness, staying compliant is crucial, especially in the contract world where you don't have a chief pilot or training department keeping track of things for you. Some key areas to stay on top of:

- Medical Certificate Renewals
- Biennial Flight Reviews (BFR) and Recurrent Training
- IFR and Night Currency

In addition to reading the current FARs, participating in industry organizations and groups like the National Business Aviation Association (NBAA) and Aircraft Owners and Pilots Association (AOPA) can help you find valuable resources that help you stay abreast of any changes in pilot currency requirements. These organizations' commentaries offer a nice alternative to reading the FARs, and in some cases, they can help explain things better.

The Value of Simulator Training and Recurrent Checks

Simulator training is where you get to make every mistake possible without actually, you know, dying. While simulator sessions can be nerve-racking, they're invaluable. They keep your skills sharp and help you prepare for real-life emergencies in a controlled environment. The bottom line is that corporate aviation is a dynamic industry that requires pilots to stay updated on best practices to maintain a high level of safety, so don't ever stop learning. Never stop training. And never stop upgrading your skills. Keep working on your craft and honing your skills. Your career, your safety, and your paycheck depend on it.

Conclusion

Getting started in corporate contract flying takes effort, investment, and a whole lot of persistence. Your medical certificate, minimum flight hours, and type ratings might seem like hurdles, but think of them as stepping stones to a career where you call the shots. Everyone's path to corporate contract flying can be a little different, but the basic starting point is to make yourself legal, eligible, and ready for hire.

Becoming a successful corporate contract pilot isn't just about logging hours in the sky; it's about mastering the business of aviation. From obtaining the right qualifications to setting up your business and ensuring your financial stability, contract flying is a path that demands skill and strategy. Contract pilots must take charge of their own professional growth by obtaining type ratings, scheduling recurrent training, and regulatory compliance. The journey starts with building your credentials—ensuring you have the required flight hours and relevant type ratings to make yourself an attractive candidate for corporate gigs. Having the right certificates alone won't cut it; you need to stay compliant with insurance companies and the FAA.

Beyond technical skills and credentials, transitioning into contract flying means stepping into the world of self-employment and business ownership. Choosing the right business structure is a crucial step in protecting yourself from liability while also ensuring your finances are handled properly. Managing your income, taxes, and deductions as a contractor requires discipline and careful planning. Corporate contract pilots must set aside funds for taxes, maintain detailed expense records, and take advantage of business write-offs to maximize their earnings. Health insurance, retirement planning, and liability protection are all part of the equation, making financial foresight an absolute necessity.

Aviation is an industry that never stops evolving, and the best contract pilots are the ones who continually upskill with new technology and tools. Stay up to speed on FAA regulations, and regularly train in simulators to keep your skills sharp. The more versatile and adaptable you are, the more valuable you become to operators looking for reliable, well-trained pilots.

At the end of the day, if you're willing to treat it like a business by staying current on training, managing your finances wisely, and marketing yourself effectively, you'll find that success isn't just about being a great pilot but about being a great entrepreneur.

CHAPTER 3

Finding Work and Building Your Network

Where to Find Contract Jobs

In the previous chapters, we discussed the qualifications and training required for becoming a contract pilot. Hopefully, you now have a solid grasp on the prerequisites of this business. Now comes the part that separates successful contract pilots from those refreshing their email inbox every five minutes, hoping for work to magically appear. Finding contract jobs, creating a strong personal brand, and developing yourself in the art of networking are the three pillars of creating continual workflow as a contractor in the corporate aviation world. Unlike airline and corporate jobs, where a neatly typed résumé and a few good interviews can land you a lifelong career, contract flying requires constant effort in marketing yourself, building relationships, and staying top-of-mind for flight departments, aircraft owners, and managers. Corporate aviation is as much about who you know as it is about what you can do in the cockpit.

This chapter will walk you through where to find contract jobs, how to create a personal brand that gets you noticed, and why networking is essential for success. We'll explore several avenues to get you booked and flying. By the time you finish this chapter, you'll know where to look for work and how to make sure people are looking for you. We're about to turn you from just another pilot looking for a job into a well-connected, high-demand aviation professional.

Job Boards, Staffing Agencies, and Direct Networking

When I first started out in contract flying, I thought the easiest way to find work would be job boards. After all, that's how most people find jobs, right? I quickly learned that while aviation job boards can be useful, they're just one piece of the puzzle. Websites like Climbto350.com, BizJetJobs.com, FindAPilot.com, and NBAA's job board do post contract pilot gigs, and they can be a good way to see what's available. In addition, In-Flight Crew Connections and Flight Crew International are some staffing agencies to check out. However, the competition is fierce, and by the time you apply, dozens of other pilots may have already thrown their hats in the ring. I am not trying to dissuade you from building your profile and brand on those sites, but you may have to dig a little deeper, too.

This is where understanding demand can help contract pilots position themselves effectively and focus their job search efforts in the right places. Your local corporate flight departments will sometimes use contract pilots to supplement their full-time crews during pilot shortages and high demand times. Charter companies and fractional ownership companies also frequently hire contractors when demand exceeds their available full-time staff. Lastly, private aircraft owners are another area where high-net-worth individuals who own private jets often seek reliable contract pilots for flexibility and availability. Knowing where demand exists can give you an edge on the competition.

Agencies like Flight Crews Unlimited, Jet Aviation Staffing, and Global Aviation Staffing all work as middlemen by connecting contract pilots with operators in need of crew. The upside is they make the heavy lifting of matching your credentials with suitable work easier, and once you've built your profile and proven yourself reliable, they'll keep calling you back. The downside is they take a cut of your pay, and weeding out work that isn't suitable can be cumbersome. However, for the new contract pilot trying to get their foot in the door, these agencies can be a good place to start. And having a steady flow of work while building your personal network is never a bad thing.

But the real gold in contract flying comes from direct networking. When you meet people in the industry, whether it's at a local FBO, a conference, or just by chatting with other pilots, you're creating potential job opportunities. I've had more gigs come from casual conversations at the airport than I ever got from job boards. Flight departments, aircraft owners, and managers love hiring pilots they know or come recommended by someone they trust. That's why building a network isn't just helpful; it's essential.

LinkedIn, Pilot Forums, and Aviation Groups

LinkedIn is the digital Rolodex for the modern professional. If you don't have a polished LinkedIn profile yet, I would seriously consider making one. It's a great way to get your name out there and build your brand. Aviation recruiters and flight department managers browse LinkedIn all the time, and if your profile isn't up to par, you could be missing out. Your profile should include a professional photo, a strong summary that highlights your experience and aircraft qualifications, and endorsements from other industry professionals. Posting about your training, certifications, and availability can also help keep you visible to the right people.

Beyond LinkedIn, pilot forums and aviation groups are great for contract work. Websites like PPRuNe and various Facebook groups dedicated to contract pilots looking for work often have job postings that don't make it to job boards (at the back of the book, I've provided a list of some of the FB groups). There seems to be fewer resources online for contract work than full-time employment, so you need to weed out the full-time stuff and focus on the gig work. These forums also serve as great places to swap advice, discuss pay rates, and learn from other pilots who've been in the game longer.

Cold Calling and Reaching Out to Operators

Cold calling sounds terrifying, right? It conjures up images of awkward phone calls, rejected emails, and politely worded "thanks, but no thanks" responses. I'm not going to lie—it does suck. I was never very good at it, but it can land you work. When reaching out to operators or flight departments, keep it short, professional, and to the point. Send a brief email first that introduces yourself, lists your aircraft qualifications, and lets them know you're available for contract work. Something as simple as:

"Hi [Chief Pilot's Name],

I'm a contract pilot typed on [Aircraft Type] based in [Location], and I'm reaching out to see if you have any upcoming needs for crew coverage. I have [X] hours in [Aircraft], and I am current on all training. I'd love to be added to your contact list for future opportunities.

Let me know if I can help or if you'd like to chat!

Best,

[Your Name]"

After sending the email, follow up with a quick phone call. If they don't need a pilot at that moment, don't take it personally—just check in every few months. I once used this type of approach, and I didn't hear anything for months. Then, out of the blue, I got a call for several days of flying. Turns out, the recipient had kept my email and reached out when he needed a contract pilot. Persistence pays off.

Also, don't underestimate the power of dropping by FBOs and introducing yourself to the people who run the show. FBOs are hubs of contract flying activity. The folks working behind the counter know which operators are frequently flying and which aircraft are in need of crew, and sometimes, they'll even pass along your name. Be friendly, leave a few business cards, and you might just land a gig. At the end of the day, finding contract work isn't about waiting for jobs to come to you; it's about putting yourself out there. Between job boards, networking groups, direct outreach, and good old-fashioned persistence, you'll eventually build a steady stream of work. And once you've built a strong reputation, you'll find that instead of searching for jobs, the jobs will start searching for you.

Creating a Strong Personal Brand

As a contract pilot, your brand is your business. Contract pilots must actively market themselves to secure opportunities. A strong personal brand sets you apart, communicates your value, and ensures you stay in demand. Building your reputation takes time, but with the right approach, you can create a brand that attracts steady work and long-term professional relationships. You can do this through developing expertise in certain aircraft, such as being the go-to guy for Learjets or Citations. It can be challenging to build a brand when you are first starting out, but it is something to keep in mind as you continue to work and develop your business. Be on the lookout for facets of the business that peak your curiosity or aspects that you can improve. Such as pain points or problems that you can solve. If you can do this, not only will this help your brand but the monetary reward can be handsome.

Crafting an Effective Aviation Résumé

When I first transitioned into contract flying, I assumed my airline experience alone would land me jobs. It didn't. My résumé, packed with flight hours and job experience, lacked personality and clarity. It wasn't until I reworked it into a concise, tailored document that it conveyed what others were looking for. Your résumé should immediately tell a chief pilot or manager why you're the best choice for their flight operation. Instead of a long-winded list of every aircraft you've ever touched, focus on what's relevant. If you're trying to land some Gulfstream flying, highlight your Gulfstream experience first. If you're new to contract flying, emphasize your adaptability, reliability, and training. Keep your résumé to one page, two at most. At the top, include your name, contact information, and certifications. Below that, list your total flight time and type ratings. Experience should come next—highlighting your most recent and relevant jobs. Finally, include education, training, and additional qualifications like international experience, crew resource management (CRM) training, or safety certifications.

One mistake I see pilots make is underselling their soft skills. Technical ability gets you in the cockpit, but your ability to work with crew members, provide excellent customer service, and handle high-pressure situations keeps you there. If you've received commendations for professionalism or teamwork, mention them. A clean, professional résumé layout can make a difference. Avoid clutter, excessive colors, or irrelevant details. And always proofread because spelling errors on a pilot résumé can make you look careless. Don't let that be you.

Building a Professional Online Presence

Again, a LinkedIn profile is arguably the most professional and important social media platform for reaching the masses. Your profile should reflect your résumé, but with more personality. Use a professional headshot if you have one. If not, use one where you're in nice clothes or aviation attire. In your headline, state your key qualifications, like "Gulfstream G650 Contract Captain | International Experience | ATP | Part 135 & 91 Ops."

The "About" section is your chance to tell your story. Why do you love corporate aviation? What makes you a great contract pilot?

Keep it concise but engaging. Use the experience section to highlight key jobs, adding descriptions that focus on your contributions rather than just listing responsibilities.

Networking is key. Connect with chief pilots, aircraft managers, owners, and fellow contract pilots. Join groups related to business aviation and participate in discussions. If you have experience with a particular aircraft type, share insights. A well-placed comment can lead to a job opportunity.

Aside from LinkedIn, consider a personal website. A simple, one-page site with your résumé, contact details, testimonials, and a few professional photos can make you stand out.

Social media can be a double-edged sword. Be mindful of what you post. Pictures of you partying in a foreign country or complaining about a previous employer can cost you opportunities. Instead, use your online presence to showcase professionalism and enthusiasm for aviation. Contribute to the aviation community with your insight on a particular subject matter you may know about.

How to Stand Out in a Competitive Industry

Contract flying is competitive, but standing out isn't just about having the most hours or training on the biggest jet. It's about reliability, attitude, and building trust. Pilots who show up on time, adapt quickly, and get along with the other crew are shoe-ins. When an organization needs a contract pilot, they call someone from that list first, before ever posting a job online. Your goal is to be on that list.

Reliability is non-negotiable. Show up early, and be ready to stay late. Have your flight plan in order, and be ready to fly. I've seen pilots lose work simply because they were late and unprepared for a trip. Aviation is a small world, and word spreads quickly. A reputation for being dependable will get you more jobs than an extra thousand hours in your logbook.

Flexibility is another key factor. The guys at the 21.Five podcast claim "flexibility is the key to airpower," and I tend to agree. Contract pilots who are willing to take last-minute trips or fill in during peak seasons build stronger relationships with operators and clients. Being available when others aren't makes you invaluable. This goes beyond availability and extends into working trips. Oftentimes, clients or passengers need to extend, leave earlier, or add an extra stop. This is when the flexibility aspect really comes into play. Don't be the guy who bucks the system because it wasn't the original plan. That will only cost you down the road.

Another way to stand out is by excelling in customer service. Corporate and charter flying often involve high-net-worth individuals who expect top-tier treatment. A pilot who knows how to interact professionally with clients, without being intrusive, can add value to any flight department. This can lead to more work. As a frontline part of the operation, be willing to grab their bags or hold the dog leash and purse during boarding. Get in the game and look for ways to help during any part of the trip. This will be remembered and appreciated. Top-tier contract pilots continuously improve their operations and are proactive about customer service.

The Power of Networking

Networking is the lifeblood of a successful career in contract flying. Contract flying relies heavily on word-of-mouth recommendations, personal connections, and industry reputation. Those who actively cultivate their network find themselves with consistent opportunities, while those who neglect it may struggle to secure work. Below are some ways to strengthen your network while building some lasting relationships.

Attending Aviation Events

Professional aviation groups are an underrated resource. Organizations like the National Business Aviation Association (NBAA), Aircraft Owners and Pilots Association (AOPA), and your local business aviation associations all hold networking events where you can rub elbows with chief pilots, recruiters, and decision-makers. These aren't just social events; they're opportunities to land your next contract gig or connect with similar people in the industry. The more people who know who you are and what you bring to the table, the more people who will think of you when work is available. Do not overlook local pilot networking gatherings and smaller regional expos, which can provide an unparalleled opportunity to make connections. These include local airport gatherings. It could be an association for the development of business aviation for the area or something as simple as a pancake breakfast. The key is to be proactive and attend. Engage and ask questions, offer insights, and follow up with the people you meet. A simple email thanking someone for their time can turn an initial conversation into a lasting professional relationship.

Maintaining Relationships

In corporate aviation, your logbook might open doors, but your relationships keep them open. The industry is small—surprisingly small. The person you flew with last month might be the chief pilot at a major flight department next year. The flight attendant you shared a layover meal with might be the one recommending pilots for an elite charter operator tomorrow. Who you know and how well you maintain those connections can determine the quality and quantity of your contract flying opportunities.

The Power of Staying Connected

A mistake many pilots make is only reaching out when they need work. That's the aviation equivalent of only calling a friend when you need to borrow their truck. People notice when you only ask for favors. Instead, treat your industry relationships like friendships—check in occasionally, congratulate a fellow pilot on a new job, share job leads with others, and offer help when you can. I have found that building relationships is the single most effective way to secure contract flying work. The corporate aviation industry thrives on trust, reputation, and word-of-mouth referrals. One pilot I know makes a habit of sending a quick text every few months to former colleagues, just to stay on their radar. A five-second message today could lead to a contract gig six months from now.

Where to Keep Relationships Warm

Industry Events & Conferences: NBAA, regional pilot meetups, and networking events are gold mines for strengthening relationships. The people you meet today might be hiring tomorrow.

Social Media & Online Groups: LinkedIn isn't just for corporate desk jockeys; aviation recruiters and operators browse it daily. Stay active, post updates, and engage with industry discussions.

Referrals & Recommendations: Recommending a fellow pilot for a gig builds goodwill and increases the odds they'll return the favor.

Staying in Touch with Former Employers and Colleagues: A pilot's previous connections—including airline coworkers, flight instructors, and maintenance personnel—can lead to referrals and job opportunities.

Conclusion

Networking isn't just about meeting people; it's about cultivating meaningful relationships that lead to future opportunities. Whether through attending industry events, building a professional online presence, or consistently demonstrating reliability and professionalism, contract pilots can create a reputation that keeps them in demand. A strong network, combined with a commitment to excellence, can turn one opportunity into a long-term, thriving career. Finding contract work requires persistence, networking, and leveraging multiple job search strategies. By building strong industry connections, utilizing online job boards, working with staffing agencies, and maintaining a professional reputation, contract pilots can create steady work for themselves.

Building a strong personal brand as a contract pilot is about creating a reputation that makes flight departments, managers, and owners want to work with you. By consistently demonstrating reliability, adaptability, and customer service skills, you can stand out in the competitive world of contract aviation.

In contract flying, your relationships are your safety net. Keep in touch, be genuinely helpful, and maintain a professional-yet-friendly presence in the industry. When opportunities arise, you want to be the first name that comes to mind. Stay connected, stay relevant, and watch how your career takes off. In the next chapter, we will explore how to negotiate rates, set pricing, and ensure financial stability with your contract flying career.

CHAPTER 4

Setting Your Rates and Negotiating Contracts

Understanding Pay Structures

One of the biggest challenges contract pilots face isn't handling crosswind landings or dealing with entitled passengers; it's figuring out what to charge. Corporate contract pilots must set their own rates, negotiate their own pay, and ensure they're actually getting paid on time. The first time I had to set my rate, I was unsure whether to charge by the hour or by the day. I quickly learned that there's no one-size-fits-all answer. It depends on the job, the client, and the overall market conditions. It's part business, part poker game, and if you don't know what you're doing, you'll end up flying for peanuts while footing your own hotel bill. The good news is with the right strategies, you can set rates that make sense, negotiate like a pro, and get paid what you deserve.

Hourly vs. Daily Rates: What's Best?

Let's start with the biggest question: Should you charge by the hour or by the day? In theory, hourly rates sound great. After all, you're getting paid for every minute you're in the air, right? But in reality, hourly rates are a trap unless you're flying back-to-back legs all day. Most corporate flying involves long waiting periods between flights, and if you're only getting paid for time in the air, you could end up spending ten hours on duty while getting paid for just three.

That's why most contract pilots opt for a daily rate. This ensures you're compensated for your entire day, not just the time spent in the cockpit. A good rule of thumb? Research the industry averages for your aircraft type and experience level. NBAA puts out an annual salary report for different types of aircraft. Chris Broyhill, a leading authority in pilot pay for the aviation industry, does a lot of research on this as well. For example, a contract captain on a Gulfstream 650 can command anywhere from $3,000 to $4000 per day, while a Citation XLS pilot might see $1,500 to $2,000 per day (2025 rates). Second-in-command (SIC) pilots earn slightly less, but even right-seaters can negotiate a solid daily rate. Of course, there are exceptions to these numbers. If you're flying a quick out-and-back or a local repositioning flight, an hourly rate might make sense or a half-day rate. The key is to factor in all the time you're committing, not just flight hours. Your commute to and from the airport, preflight, and postflight should be considered.

Per Diems and Travel Reimbursements

Most operators cover expenses incurred during the trip, such as hotel, meals, and ground transportation, but the way they handle these expenses varies. Some offer a flat per diem per day. Others reimburse actual expenses with receipts. There are pros and cons to both. A per diem is great if you're thrifty and can eat for cheap, but if you're stuck in an overpriced area with twenty-dollar sandwiches, you might burn through your per diem fast. Reimbursement for actual expenses ensures you're covered, but tracking receipts is a pain (and some companies take forever to process reimbursements). Clarify your policy upfront so you don't end up paying out of pocket, and always clarify travel reimbursements before accepting a trip.

Hotels and transportation should also be addressed. Will the client book your hotel, or will you need to cover it and submit receipts for reimbursement? Will ground transportation be arranged, or will you need to rent a car? These details may seem minor at first, but over the course of multiple trips, they can add up significantly. Most operators expect that you will book your rental car, hotel, airfare, or ride to/from the FBO. There's nothing worse than landing at 1 a.m. in a town with no Ubers and realizing you're stranded, so I usually take care of booking whatever I need for the trip in advance. You will want a rental car on a multi-day trip, whereas on day trips, you can get by with a crew car, Uber, and meal delivery services. You'll generally book airfare and hotels yourself, since you are the one taking the flight or sleeping in that hotel. So don't let anyone dictate that without your consent—OK?

How to Negotiate Your Contracts

Once you've determined your rates and figured out how to handle your expenses, the next challenge is negotiating a fair contract that protects both you and your client. Contracts are more than just agreements on pay. They outline expectations, responsibilities, and liabilities. Understanding key clauses can help prevent misunderstandings and protect you from legal risks.

Key Clauses to Look For in Agreements

You want to make sure your contract has a clear job scope. A vague contract can lead to unrealistic expectations, so I always ensure that flight duty days are spelled out. Flight hours, duty hours, and cancellation policies are explicitly stated. Scheduling conflicts will arise, and the client's expectations need to be garnered with clear language from your contract. I now make sure every agreement includes defined duty hours, compensation for overage, and a clear cancellation policy.

Avoiding Common Pitfalls and Legal Risks

Another critical area to watch out for is liability and indemnification. You should be able to find clients that either name you on their insurance policy, or you may meet the open pilot clause with the insurance company with your flight time and experience. Be leery if a client tries to include clauses that shift excessive liability onto you. I would pass on those gigs. If you have to include some language to appease the client, keep it simple, like a clause stating "gross negligence or willful misconduct," ensuring that you are not unfairly held accountable for things beyond your control. Common sense prevails here and if you need a second opinion, resources such as AOPA legal services can help.

When to Walk Away from a Bad Deal

A good contract pilot is also a savvy business operator who knows how to protect their time, maximize their earnings, and ensure they get paid what they're worth. Corporate contract flying offers incredible flexibility and earning potential, but only if you treat it like a business. Know your worth, stand firm on your terms, and don't let a lowball offer tempt you into flying for less than you deserve. The skies are full of opportunities, but only for those who navigate them wisely. Negotiating contracts is about balancing confidence with flexibility. By understanding key contract clauses, spotting red flags, and knowing when to walk away, contract pilots can protect themselves while securing fair, professional agreements.

Payment Terms and Invoicing Best Practices

Getting paid as a contract pilot isn't always as straightforward as collecting a paycheck. Without a structured payroll system, you're responsible for invoicing clients and ensuring timely payment. Learning the ins and outs of invoicing and payment terms is just as important as negotiating your rate.

So you've set your rate, negotiated your expenses and contract, and completed the flight. Now comes the fun part: getting paid. Here's the harsh reality: Not every client pays on time. Some are great and process payments within a week. Others act like it's the last thing on their mind. If you don't establish clear payment terms, you could wait months. Not good. Invoicing should be simple and professional. I use an invoice template that includes my name, business entity (if applicable), contact information, flight dates, agreed-upon rate, and any reimbursable expenses. Clear and well-organized invoices help prevent delays and ensure smooth transactions. Additionally, I send a follow-up email a few days prior to an invoice reaching the agreed-upon payment deadline to mitigate a late payment penalty.

The best way to avoid late payment is to provide your payment terms upfront. They should be clearly laid out in your contract, mentioned in any email correspondence, and included on your invoice. Most contract pilots require payment within seven to fourteen days. Anything beyond thirty days is penalized with a late fee on the following invoice. Some pilots even require a partial deposit upfront for new clients, which isn't a bad idea if you're flying for someone you've never worked with before. I generally give everyone the benefit of the doubt and have not tried to bill anything prior to the trip.

Your invoice should include:

- Your name and business entity (LLC if you have one)
- The flight dates and aircraft type flown
- Your daily rate or total fee
- Any reimbursable expenses (attach receipts if needed)
- Payment terms and due date
- Your banking details for wire transfer or preferred payment method

Some pilots prefer old-school paper invoices, but digital invoicing software like QuickBooks, Wave, or even a simple PDF template can speed up payments. And always send a follow-up email if payment is late. A polite nudge like, "Hey [Client], just following up on my invoice from [Flight Date]. Let me know if you need any additional details!" usually does the trick. If not, a firmer reminder might be necessary. Electronic payments are now the norm, but it's still important to discuss payment methods ahead of time. Some companies prefer bank transfers, while others use payment platforms like PayPal, Venmo, or direct deposit.

And here's a final tip: Keep records of everything. If you ever have to chase down a late payment, having a clear email trail showing your agreement, invoice, and follow-ups makes it much easier to demand what you're owed.

Understanding pay structures and setting clear financial expectations can make all the difference in a contract pilot's career. By learning from my early mistakes and refining my approach to rate-setting, travel reimbursements, and invoicing, I've been able to build a sustainable and profitable career. Setting your rates and negotiating contracts as a corporate pilot is part art and part science. Charge too little, and you'll be overworked and underpaid. Charge too much, and you might price yourself out of jobs. Finding that sweet spot takes research, confidence, and experience. Always factor in your time, expenses, and training costs when setting your rate. In the next section, we'll dive into the art of negotiation—how to confidently discuss rates, advocate for fair compensation, and secure long-term contracts that benefit pilots and clients.

Maximizing Your Earnings

There are a few ways to increase earnings as a contract pilot. One is to actively enhance your marketability. And one of the more effective ways to do this is by specializing in high-demand aircraft types, as we discussed in Chapter 2. Obtaining type ratings in these aircraft makes you a more valuable asset to operators and private owners. Another key strategy is securing repeat clients. I have found that operators and private jet owners prefer working with familiar pilots whom they trust. By consistently demonstrating professionalism, flexibility, and strong customer service, you can become the preferred choice for a particular client. One of my most consistent contract gigs started when I filled in for a last-minute trip. I made sure to arrive early, handle every detail smoothly, and follow up with a thank-you email after the trip. That one flight turned into a long-term working relationship that still provides steady work to this day, years later.

How to Increase Your Value as a Pilot

Building relationships with flight departments and managers is another way to secure repeat business. Staying in touch, keeping your availability updated, and delivering excellent service every time ensures that you remain on the top of their call list when opportunities arise. Don't just be a pilot—be a damn good one. Show up prepared, be professional, and make life easy for the people hiring you. When you are at work, look for work. This may sound obvious, but I see guys unwilling to grab a bag, clean a windscreen, hold a door, or take care of other small tasks that need doing. This is your opportunity to go the extra mile and up your customer service game. Cool the cabin down prior to passengers arriving, have some cold water in the cup holders, and have any other preferences teed up in the cabin. As Roger Staubach said, "There is no traffic jam along the extra mile."

Specializing in High-Demand Aircraft Types

Seeking employment in aircraft that are always in demand is a great strategy for ensuring steady work. When you focus on aircraft that are in high demand, you can increase your ability to earn. These are not always the sexiest aircraft, but they are prevalent throughout the industry and often need pilots. I mention this because I want you to be aware that there are solid money-making opportunities outside of the larger bizjet that you may be aspiring to. We all tend to think bigger airplanes, more money. And, in some cases this is true, but being proficient and current in a high-demand aircraft can be a goldmine for you.

Strategies for Securing Repeat Clients

Lastly, treat every flight like a long-term job interview. Clients remember pilots who go the extra mile, whether that's remembering their coffee order or ensuring the jet's cabin is immaculate before they board. A great reputation means repeat business, higher rates, and fewer nights spent wondering where your next paycheck is coming from. In short, be the pilot everyone wants to hire, and you'll never be out of work.

Conclusion

Setting your rates and negotiating contracts as a contract pilot means being business savvy and knowing when to walk away from a bad deal. It's a skill that improves with experience, but one thing is certain: If you don't set your value, someone else will—and it won't be in your favor. You're not just selling a day of flying; you're selling safety, expertise, reliability, and the ability to keep passengers happy while ensuring smooth operations. Understanding different pay structures, from daily rates to per-diems and reimbursements, allows you to maximize your earnings while keeping your finances predictable. Smart contract pilots don't just take what's offered; they negotiate confidently, knowing that a well-structured contract means fewer headaches and more money in the bank. But even more important than getting paid well is getting paid on time.

Establishing clear payment terms, invoicing professionally, and standing firm when a client tries to push payment out an extra thirty days ensures that you're not chasing down money for months after the trip.

The contract flying world is full of opportunity, but those who treat it like a business—not just a job—are the ones who thrive. Maximizing your earnings isn't about luck; it's about increasing your value as a pilot, specializing in high-demand aircraft, and securing repeat clients who see you as indispensable. The pilots who stay consistently booked aren't necessarily the best aviators in the sky; they're the ones who show up prepared, act professionally, and make themselves the easiest choice when a client needs a trusted pilot. Building long-term relationships with operators, managers, and aircraft owners means that instead of hunting for work, work comes to you. At the heart of contract flying success is the ability to know your worth, stand by it, and walk away from deals that don't align with your expertise or financial goals. There will always be lowball offers, clients who try to squeeze every dollar out of you, and jobs that sound too good to be true. But when you set clear boundaries, negotiate smartly, and prove your value on every trip, you create a sustainable and profitable contract career.

CHAPTER 5

Mastering the Corporate Aviation Experience

What Corporate Clients Expect from You

Flying for corporate clients isn't just about nailing greaser landings and remembering to turn off the seatbelt sign before the boss stands up. It is its own unique circus, and as a contract pilot, you are both the ringleader and the lion tamer. The secret to success is professionalism, discretion, and making sure your passengers feel like royalty, all while staying flexible and maintaining a positive mental attitude. If those things sound like things you can handle, then you will be in good shape.

Professionalism and Discretion in Private Aviation

When you fly for a private jet owner, an executive team, or some hedge-fund wizard who makes more in a minute than you do in a year, professionalism is going to be required. And by professionalism, I don't mean just wearing a sharp uniform and keeping your hair brushed (though that helps). I mean becoming the James Bond of the flight deck—calm, competent, and completely unflappable even when your client or passengers are asking you to do things that defy safety or FAA regulations.

One time, I had a client ask if we could extend the duty day a little longer, which became outside of my comfort level given the current circumstances. As much as I would've loved to have accommodated him and secured my place as his favorite pilot, I had to politely explain that if he had arrived on time, we wouldn't be up against time constraints and foul weather. The key is saying no without ever actually saying no. "I'll see what I can do" is often the best response, even when you know full well what they're asking is not feasible. A lot of times, things work themselves out without you having to be the bad guy.

Then there's discretion. If you have even the slightest tendency toward gossip, corporate aviation will beat it out of you quickly. What happens on the jet stays on the jet. You will see things personal, professional, and sometimes just downright bizarre. But you don't react. You don't stare. You simply greet them, close the door, and pretend this is exactly the level of normal you expected. Your job is to be an unshakable professional, no matter how ridiculous the situation becomes.

Providing VIP Service Beyond Just Flying

If you think your only job as a corporate contract pilot is to get from Point A to Point B safely, you might want to reconsider how you view this gig. Flying is about 30 percent of the job, and the other 70 percent consists of customer service, logistics, and making sure your passengers have the best experience possible. You're not just the pilot. You're often also a concierge, a problem-solver, and occasionally, a therapist.

You will have passengers request that you book their rental car or coordinate their ground transportation. You will receive requests for specific food and beverages to be on board. It could be anything

63

from a specific catering request to ensuring there are no foods that pose the risk for a severe allergic reaction on board. Overlooking the latter will get you busy pretty quickly. Most clients are reasonable to work with, but on occasion, you will have an unusual request. Again, just roll with it, and do your best. In this world, the type of peanuts onboard may matter more than departure times, and the specific type of rental car requested should be standing by on arrival.

And it's not just about food and beverages. Everything about the flight experience needs to be seamless. The cabin should be spotless, the temperature exactly how they like it, and the Wi-Fi should work as well as possible. Paying attention to the little things will make you memorable. Greet them by name, help with boarding, and make sure the cabin is set up correctly. Corporate passengers want effortless luxury, the feeling that everything has been arranged to their liking before they even ask.

Handling High-Net-Worth Individuals and Executives

Flying high-net-worth individuals and executives is like entering an alternate dimension where time is money, money is infinite, and waiting five extra minutes for catering is a personal affront to their very existence. Sometimes you are flying people who are used to the world bending to their every whim, and while most are perfectly pleasant, others may test the limits of your patience and professionalism.

One of my first flights as a contract pilot was for a CEO who could not maintain a schedule. He was so late that I thought the flight had been cancelled without my knowledge. After a couple of hours of waiting with no word, I started putting the plane away. Next thing I knew, here he came, barreling in on two wheels, jumping out, and apologizing. We went ahead with the mission as planned, but it was a real eye-opener to me.

Executives and high-net-worth individuals expect efficiency, but they also expect unquestionable competence. They don't want excuses; they want solutions. If there's a delay, they expect you to handle it before they even know it's a problem. If there's a change in plans, they want you to adjust immediately, without hesitation. By all means, keep them in the loop; just know that this is the expectation.

You must stay ahead of their needs at all times. Anticipate problems before they arise. If there's weather en route, have a backup plan ready. If they need to be in a meeting the second they land, coordinate ground transportation to be standing by with an in-range call to the FBO.

Adapting to Different Flight Departments

If contract flying were a game show, it would be called Welcome to a New Flight Department, Now Figure Everything Out Before Takeoff. One day, you're working with a sleek, well-organized operation where everything runs like a Swiss watch. The next day, you're walking into what can only be described as organized chaos, wondering if the company's safety procedures were written on the back of a cocktail napkin. The ability to adapt quickly to different flight departments, policies, crew dynamics, and aircraft operations will be essential to your survival. Here are a few tips to help you navigate.

Differences in Policies and Procedures

Walking into a new flight department for the first time is a lot like meeting your in-laws: you're not sure what the rules are, you don't know who's in charge, and at some point, someone is going to judge you for how you handle a difficult situation. The policies and procedures at each flight department can vary wildly. Some have thick manuals detailing every possible contingency, while others operate on a "just do what makes sense" philosophy, which is both freeing and terrifying.

I've flown for corporate operations where every detail was thoroughly documented, complete with layers of checks and balances. Meanwhile, my inbox would fill with emails about the trip, each requiring a response. At times, I spent more hours on the preflight logistics than on the actual flight. On the opposite end of the spectrum, I've had an aircraft manager casually hand me the keys, point to the jet on the ramp, and ask, "You good?" The difference between the two approaches can be jarring.

As a contract pilot, you have to be a chameleon. If the department is structured and detail-oriented, you follow their checklist to the letter. If they operate more loosely, you have to rely on your judgment while still ensuring you maintain safety and industry standards. The key is knowing how to read the room, figure out how things are done, ask smart questions without calling people out, and adapt on the fly, literally.

Crew Dynamics and Working with Different Teams

There are few things in life more unpredictable than walking into a flight department and meeting your new crew member for the day.

Some teams click instantly, working together like a championship basketball team. Others feel more like an awkward first date where no one is sure what to say, and you just hope nobody does anything too embarrassing.

One time, I arrived at a gig expecting to fly right seat with a seasoned captain. Instead, I found myself paired with a guy who introduced himself with a long sigh and the phrase, "Well, I guess we're doing this." Confidence-inspiring, right? By the time we were taxiing out, I had learned three crucial facts about him: he despised flying at night, he believed he should have stayed with his first wife, and he had an unhealthy attachment to a substandard hotel chain for overnights. I can remember contemplating my career choices that day.

In corporate aviation, crew dynamics are unpredictable, and you have to be able to get along with everyone from ex-military hardliners who jerk the flight controls around like Maverick to the young, inexperienced guys you have to watch like a hawk. Some pilots and flight departments will treat you like an equal from the start, while others will make you feel like the new guy. Your job is to blend in, be easy to work with, and not cause drama.

Communication is key. Every crew has different habits. Some captains brief every leg in meticulous detail, while others will give you the "as previously briefed." If you don't know what their style is, ask. A simple "Hey, how do you like to do things?" can save you from mid-flight surprises. And never assume anything. Just because you did something a certain way with your last crew doesn't mean it's how things are done here. Soft skills and people skills are just as important as good CRM in the cockpit.

How to Quickly Adjust to New Aircraft and Operations

There is nothing quite as humbling as sitting in the cockpit of an aircraft you're typed in but haven't flown in a while; finding things on the panel may be like an Easter egg hunt. Your ability to jump into a new cockpit and get up to speed quickly is a valuable skill as a contract pilot.

The trick is to always be prepared. Before any new gig, I do a quick refresher on the aircraft. This usually involves digging out my old training manuals or watching YouTube tutorials on programming an FMS I haven't used in a while. If I am lucky, I can get to the aircraft earlier than normal and acquaint myself with the cockpit layout. If not, all is not lost; it's just going to take a little more time than normal.

Some aircraft are easy to transition between. If you've flown one Citation Jet (CJ), flying another is mostly a matter of adjusting to a few different switches and flows. But jump from a King Air to a Learjet, and suddenly, it's like going from driving a Honda Civic to piloting a space shuttle. Beyond the aircraft, you also have to adapt to the specific operations of each flight department. Some places expect pilots to handle everything, while others have teams dedicated to making sure you never lift anything heavier than a headset. No matter the situation, act like you belong. Even if you feel like you're in over your head, confidence is key. Review the aircraft systems, pay attention to the flow of operations, and follow the lead of the regular pilots if you are working in a crew environment.

Ensuring a Seamless Flight Experience

Flying the plane is easy. Making sure everything leading up to that flight runs smoothly can be the real challenge. Running a trip as a contract pilot is less about stick-and-rudder skills and more about mastering the art of logistics, diplomacy, and keeping your cool when everything inevitably goes sideways. A successful contract pilot ensures every part of the experience is seamless, from the moment the trip is scheduled to the second the passengers step off the plane. You must handle pre-flight planning like a pro, calmly adapt to last-minute itinerary changes, and solve problems under pressure like you're starring in an aviation-themed action movie.

Pre-Flight Planning and International Ops Considerations

We have discussed some pre-flight planning, duties, and expectations thus far, but in corporate aviation, it is a lot more hands-on. Unlike the airlines—where dispatchers hand you a neatly organized flight plan, passenger manifest, and weight balance with your fuel load—contract pilots are often responsible for every detail, and it's on you to make sure no one ends up stranded in a foreign country because you forgot to check visa requirements.

I learned this lesson the hard way on an international trip early in my contract flying career. We were scheduled for a simple hop from the U.S. to the Caribbean, typically an easy day's work. Ten minutes before departure, there was a planeside break-up, so one of the passengers would no longer be making the trip. I rushed inside the FBO to make the necessary changes to the international manifest and resubmit it to U.S. Customs. By the time I resubmitted the new manifest and got back out to the plane, I discovered they had magically patched things up, and now she was going on the flight. Here I am, silently swearing to never work for this client again while redoing the necessary international manifest, adding her back on the flight. All normal stuff.

International ops come with their own unique challenges. Customs, overflight permits, fuel availability, and handling fees all vary depending on where you're flying, and you can't afford to assume that yesterday's rules still apply today. There are places where a landing permit takes two minutes to secure, and there are places where it requires a fourteen-page application, three separate fees, and a personal blessing from a government official who may or may not be on vacation. The key is meticulous planning, starting the planning early, and having a network of great handlers who can bail you out when you inevitably miss something. The use of a handler is a good plan if you are new to international ops.

Managing Last-Minute Itinerary Changes

I touched on this in the aforementioned love story, but if you hate uncertainty, surprises, or rich people who suddenly decide they need to be somewhere else "right now," then contract flying might not be for you. One of the biggest differences between airline and corporate flying is that in corporate aviation, the schedule is written in pencil, and it will change. You can file your flight plan, brief your crew member, and have everything set up perfectly, only to receive a call five minutes before departure informing you that the boss now wants to go somewhere completely different.

Some situations will require a combination of quick thinking, diplomacy, and an ability to coordinate logistics at the speed of light. Calling the FBO to check ground transportation availability, adjusting fuel loads, ensuring performance numbers are safe for a change of destination, and coordinating with ATC all need to happen. The secret to managing these last-minute changes? Always assume they're going to happen. Have backup plans in place. Know the alternates along your route. Learn how to interact with FBO customer service reps so you can work miracles when needed.

Problem-Solving in High-Pressure Situations

If you work this gig long enough, something will go wrong. It's not a question of if; it's a question of when and how spectacularly. A good contract pilot will be poised and handle those moments when things start to fall apart.

The best thing you can do is stay calm, proactive, and adaptable. Whether it's a maintenance issue, a last-minute schedule change, or a passenger who suddenly insists on bringing a large, uncrated dog on board (it's happened), your ability to handle stress with humor and confidence will set you apart and protect your sanity. This is also a chance for you to show your soft skills and manage the unpredictable. I assure you, this will not be lost on the clients. They will likely notice this and respect your poise. This could lead to the beginning of a longer relationship where you are requested to fly them again in the future.

Conclusion

Adapting to different flight departments is both an art and a skill. Some days, you'll feel like a seasoned pro, effortlessly blending into a new operation. Other days, you'll be convinced that the airplane, the crew, and the universe itself are conspiring against you. The keys are maintaining flexibility, professionalism, and a willingness to learn.

A seamless flight experience is about far more than just flying the airplane. It's about meticulous pre-flight planning, gracefully handling last-minute changes during the operation, and solving problems before they turn into disasters.

Every trip is a new puzzle to solve, and while you can't plan for every scenario, you can develop the mindset and skills to handle whatever comes your way. So, the next time your flight plan gets thrown out the window, your passengers change destinations at the last second, or your aircraft starts acting in a way it absolutely should not, just take a deep breath, think clearly, and remember: if you can keep calm and touch down safely, you're already ahead of the game.

CHAPTER 6

Managing Your Schedule and Work–Life Balance

How to Stay Consistently Booked Without Overworking

One of the biggest paradoxes in contract flying is that success brings more work but too much work leads to burnout, bad decision-making, and the kind of stress that makes you wonder why you ever left that airline job with a steady schedule and free buddy passes. Figuring out how to stay consistently booked without working yourself into an early grave is a challenge in corporate aviation. You don't want to be the pilot who's constantly scrambling for work, nor do you want to be the one who's so overloaded with trips that you have no time for relaxation and your dog has forgotten who you are. The goal is to find that sweet spot where you are busy enough to make great money, but not so busy that you compromise your personal relationships and commitments.

Balancing Short-Term Gigs with Long-Term Contracts

Short-term gigs and long-term contracts are like the dating scene of corporate aviation—one is exciting but unpredictable, while the other is stable but comes with its own challenges. Let's look at how to balance the two and what challenges each one poses.

Short-term gigs such as one-off trips or a few days of flying here and there are great because they keep your schedule flexible and your earnings high. One month, you might be bouncing between three different operators, racking up flight hours and making great connections. The next month, you might find yourself with a schedule so erratic that you are struggling to stay caught up. The upside is big paychecks and lots of variety. The downside is you're constantly hustling for the next gig.

On the other hand, long-term contracts offer stability but come with the risk of complacency and limitations on other work opportunities. Some contract pilots take on three- to six-month gigs with a single flight department or aircraft owner, which provides steady income and some predictability. The challenge is that long-term contracts can prevent you from taking higher-paying one-off jobs when they pop up. Being stuck in a commitment just as a better-paying gig opens up stings.

Doug Carmody, in The Contract Pilot's Handbook, emphasizes the importance of strategic scheduling—he suggests finding a mix of "anchor clients" (reliable long-term contracts) and "opportunistic jobs" (high-paying one-offs). The key is to structure your work so you have some predictability, but enough flexibility to take advantage of lucrative opportunities when they arise. Think of it as building a financial safety net while keeping room for the occasional high-dollar windfall. I tend to agree with Doug on this and think that it is a good approach between the two.

Avoiding Common Scheduling Mistakes

Every contract pilot has a horror story about overbooking themselves, double-scheduling flights, or realizing mid-month that they haven't had a day off in weeks. I once booked back-to-back trips with different clients, only to discover at the last minute that I had to be in two places at the same time. Through some diplomatic crow-eating, I was able to fulfill both obligations. Lesson learned: Don't assume your future self will magically "figure out" scheduling conflicts. Use a calendar, and keep it up to date. Train yourself to go to it every time a trip request comes up before committing. Additionally, use it to note the times when you are unavailable. Put your personal commitments on it as well. This may sound trivial, but it certainly wasn't second nature to me initially. Over time, it has helped me avoid some of those early scheduling mistakes.

Another potential scheduling mistake is saying yes to everything. I am guilty of this as well. It's easy to fall into the trap of accepting every trip that comes your way, especially when business is booming. But this could lead to exhaustion and personal scheduling conflicts.

A few golden rules to avoid schedule disasters:

- Use a solid digital calendar system religiously. If you're still keeping track of flights in a notebook, it's only a matter of time before you miss a trip.
- Don't book flights back-to-back without careful consideration. If a job runs late, you don't want to be explaining to another client why you can't make their departure time.

75

- Leave room for yourself. A day off here and there will do wonders for your mental and physical health. It's hard to be an elite contract pilot if you're running on fumes and bad coffee.

- Remember the word "no" is a complete sentence. Don't be afraid to use it.

Good contract pilots learn to work smart and manage their time efficiently. They know when to say no, and they work to avoid the panic-driven chaos of last-minute schedule shuffling.

Managing Slow Periods and Securing Future Work

Even the best contractors experience slow periods. There will be months when you're booked solid, and others where your phone is as silent as a deserted airport at 2 a.m. The key to surviving slow seasons is planning ahead, maintaining relationships, and keeping your marketing game strong.

I have noticed a lot of new contract pilots only network when they need work. The best pilots will build and maintain connections year-round, even when they're swamped. Keep in touch with operators, aircraft managers, owners, and fellow pilots. Send a quick check-in email, comment on LinkedIn posts, or even just grab a coffee with an industry contact. When the slow season comes, you'll still be connected to your contacts and in a position to benefit when work picks up again. If you only reach out when you're desperate, people can sense it. So keep relationships warm, and you will be the first person they call when they need a pilot.

Another key to surviving slow seasons? Diversify your income streams. Some contract pilots teach on the side, do ferry flights, or even offer consulting for aircraft owners. If you can find a way to make money in aviation beyond just flying, you'll be in a much better position when flying work slows down. Plus, it keeps you from making questionable financial decisions when you realize you haven't had a trip in two weeks. More on this in Chapter 8.

Staying Healthy on the Road

Corporate aviation is many things, but a lifestyle that promotes peak physical and mental health is not one of them. Between the fatigue, the weird sleep hours, the endless string of hotel rooms, and the siren call of fast food, staying healthy on the road can feel like an Olympic event. But unless you want to be the guy who gets winded walking up the airstairs or who needs three cups of coffee just to turn on the avionics, figuring out how to take care of yourself on the road is going to be essential. Staying healthy as a contract pilot is about managing fatigue, staying active, and finding ways to eat something that didn't come out of a drive-thru bag. I could write a whole book on this, but I'll keep it to a couple of key ideas.

Managing Fatigue and Irregular Sleep Schedules

The phrase "pilot fatigue" sounds like the title of a 1950s aviation training film where a square-jawed captain heroically fights off exhaustion while saving his aircraft from imminent disaster. In reality, pilot fatigue is less about dramatic mid-air emergencies and more about trying to function like a human being when your circadian rhythm has been reduced to rubble. The irregular schedules of corporate aviation mean that sometimes you're up at dawn, sometimes you're flying late into the night, and sometimes you're sitting at an airport lounge wondering why you feel so tired.

One tip for managing fatigue is learning to sleep whenever and wherever you can. This may mean power naps in FBO crew lounges or melatonin-assisted time zone adjustments (if you go this route, do it with caution). It also helps to avoid the classic mistake of thinking you'll "catch up on sleep later." You won't. Later never comes. Another strategy that I like is to set yourself a consistent bedtime when you can. The earlier the better. Although this isn't popular when you're on an overnight with another crew member, it will ensure that you have at least positioned yourself to get some quality rest. You'll thank me when the doors start slamming shut in the hotel because the railroaders are going to work at 3 a.m., and you've been in bed since 8 p.m. Additionally, if you have downtime, use it wisely, because you never know when or where your next full night's sleep will be.

Staying Active While Traveling

Staying fit as a contract pilot is an ongoing battle against inertia, fatigue, and the deep-seated temptation to collapse into a hotel bed and remain there until your next flight. The combination of long flights, waiting around in FBOs, and spending your nights in hotels does not lend itself to an active lifestyle. I once went through a particularly busy stretch of flying where I realized I had not walked more than five hundred steps in three days. That's not "staying active." That's "slowly turning into furniture."

The good news is that staying active on the road doesn't require a gym membership or a personal trainer—just a little creativity and a willingness to look mildly ridiculous in public places. Hotel gyms are often sad little rooms with a broken treadmill, a set of dumbbells, and a bike, but a workout is a workout. If that's all you've got, use it.

If the hotel gym is truly a lost cause, improvise. Throw on some sneakers and walk around outside. If you're in an FBO with an empty ramp, take a brisk walk around the aircraft (just don't make it look like you're casing the joint). If you're really ambitious, bodyweight exercises in your hotel room are an option, though if you are going to do push-ups next to the bed, please put a towel down. But the best way to stay active on the road? Get outside. If you have a long layover or a day off between flights, find a nearby park, rent a bike, or just explore the city on foot. Not only will you get some exercise, but you'll also avoid spending yet another day in a hotel room, staring at the Weather Channel, and burning zero calories.

Eating Well and Maintaining Mental Well-Being

The sheer number of bad food choices available to pilots on the road is staggering. Every airport and FBO is a gauntlet of greasy food, sugary snacks, and enough caffeine options to keep a freight pilot awake for a week. It is incredibly easy to fall into the habit of eating whatever is fast and available, which is why so many pilots have diets that would make a nutritionist weep.

One trick to eating well on the road is planning ahead and making smarter choices when you can. If you have time before a flight, grab a real meal instead of relying on FBO vending machines. Stock up on healthy snacks like protein bars, meat sticks/jerky, or any other whole food options. Ensure you're not at the mercy of whatever deep-fried monstrosity is available at the next stop. Hydration is another key. It's easy to forget to drink water when you're running on coffee and adrenaline, but dehydration just makes fatigue worse.

I recently succumbed to a carnivore-type approach to my diet while on the road due to decision fatigue. A three-day trip can mean deciding where and what to eat nine times in seventy-two hours. I just couldn't keep making those choices over and over. Just find some meat, eat it, and move on. I try to avoid carbs and sugars on the road. Only time will tell if this proves to be a healthy approach, but I do love reducing the number of decisions to be made while at work. Dr. Ken Berry has done a lot of research on this type of diet if you are inclined to learn more.

As for mental well-being? That's just as important as physical health. The combination of long hours, stress, and constant travel can take its toll, so finding ways to decompress is essential. Some pilots swear by meditation apps, others by podcasts, and some just need a solid hour of mindless TV at the end of the day. Whatever keeps you sane, make time for it. And keep in mind that alcohol is not exactly a performance drink. It often leads to a reduction in mental well-being.

The biggest mental health tip is to keep a sense of humor. If you can't laugh at the absurdity of corporate aviation, you're going to have a rough time. When you find yourself explaining to a hotel front desk that, yes, you need a late checkout and a room away from the elevator because you just got in so late, embrace the ridiculousness. It's all part of the adventure.

Maintaining Personal and Family Life

Contract flying is a strange and wonderful existence. One moment, you're waking up in a five-star hotel with a view of the ocean, sipping an espresso like you belong in a travel magazine. Next, you're sleeping in a courtesy car parked behind an FBO because your hotel won't let you check-in until 3 p.m. and you're too tired to argue with the front desk. Balancing personal and family life with this nomadic career takes more than just good intentions; it requires boundaries, effort, and the ability to keep your loved ones' minds at ease.

Setting Boundaries with Clients and Work Commitments

One of the greatest traps in contract flying is the illusion of infinite availability with clients. If you say yes to every trip, every last-minute request, and every "just one more leg" extension, you'll eventually find yourself staring into the void of burnout while eating your fourth consecutive airport sandwich. Worse, you'll train clients to assume you have no personal life, which means they'll call at all hours, assuming you'll drop everything to fly their dog to Aspen.

I once had a client call me at 10 p.m. on a Tuesday, asking if I could commute out that evening to be in position for a flight the next morning. This was a flight that hadn't even been mentioned before. No schedule, no warning, just a "Hey, can you do this?" as if I were waiting by my phone, fully dressed, just hoping someone

81

would need me. I realized I had failed at setting boundaries with clients.

Boundaries are not just important; they are survival skills. Like we discussed before, the key is learning to say no without sounding like a jerk. It's about making it clear that, yes, you are available—but on your terms. If a client calls at an unreasonable hour, let it go to voicemail. If they insist on last-minute trips with no consideration for your schedule, politely but firmly remind them that you require proper notice. And when you do take time off, commit to it. No "just this one more quick flight," and no allowing clients to think they can talk you into working when you've already said no. Once you let them cross the line, it's difficult to get things back in check.

Keeping Relationships Strong Despite a Nomadic Lifestyle

Being a contract pilot means learning to maintain relationships in nontraditional ways. You're gone for days at a time, you miss birthdays, anniversaries, and major life events, and sometimes, your most meaningful conversations with loved ones happen over terrible hotel Wi-Fi. If you're not careful, your family starts to feel more like people you send postcards to rather than the ones you share a life with.

Early in my contract career, I thought "quality over quantity" would be enough—I figured that as long as I was fully present when I was home, it wouldn't matter how often I was gone. The secret to keeping relationships strong while living life in the air is active effort. It's about making it count. If you're away, call, text, and video chat regularly. If you're home, be home. Don't spend your time off catching up on paperwork or saying yes to "just one more trip." Plan things ahead of time. Book vacations, set date nights, and don't let your schedule become a running excuse for why you're never around. Also, always communicate clearly to your family about when you're coming home.

Strategies for Taking Real Time Off

If you don't schedule your time, someone else will do it for you. One of the more common pitfalls with contract flying is the idea that you can rest later. You think, "I'll just take one more trip, and then I'll take a break." But then another trip comes up. And another. And suddenly, you're in a three-week stretch of nonstop work.

I once made the mistake of not blocking off vacation time in advance, assuming I'd just "find a break" somewhere. The result? I worked myself into exhaustion, and when I finally tried to take time off, I had so many clients expecting me to be available that I spent most of my "vacation" answering phone calls. Lesson learned: if you don't put your own time off on the calendar, no one else will.

Taking real time off is treating it like an ironclad commitment. Block it out months in advance. Tell your clients and your family, and most importantly, respect your own boundaries. When a trip offer inevitably comes up during your scheduled break, remind yourself that rest is just as important as revenue. No one flies well when they're running on fumes. Taking time off also means actually disconnecting. Turn off your work phone. Ignore emails. Resist the urge to "check in" on things. If you don't, you'll spend your entire vacation mentally back in the cockpit, stressing about flights you're not even flying. Your clients will survive without you for a week. I promise.

Conclusion

Managing your schedule and work-life balance as a contract pilot isn't just about knowing when to take trips—it's about knowing which trips to take, how to structure your calendar, and when to turn down work to avoid burnout.

Balancing short-term gigs with long-term contracts ensures a steady income while leaving room for high-paying opportunities. Avoid scheduling disasters by planning ahead, maintaining realistic buffers, and knowing when to say no. Contract flying is a marathon, not a sprint. If you try to book yourself non-stop, you'll burn out faster than a cheap headset battery. But if you learn to manage your time wisely, you can create a career that's lucrative and sustainable. A career that allows you to fly great aircraft, work with incredible clients, and actually have a life outside of the cockpit. What's the point of making great money if you're too tired to enjoy it?

Staying healthy on the road as a contract pilot is about balance and discipline, and sometimes, a bit of luck. Managing fatigue means prioritizing sleep whenever you can. Staying active requires creativity and a willingness to move, even when it's difficult. Eating well means making the best choices available.

Most importantly, don't take yourself too seriously. No matter how much planning you do, there will be days when you sleep in an airport lounge, eat something questionable, and get zero exercise. That's fine. Just don't let one bad day turn into a bad habit. Stay proactive, stay adaptable, and when in doubt, drink more water and get outside.

Managing your personal and family life as a contract pilot isn't just about balance. It's about setting priorities, drawing boundaries, and making sure the people in your life don't start referring to you as "that person who occasionally visits." It's about protecting your time, keeping your relationships strong, and making sure your career doesn't turn into a 24/7 job that consumes everything else.

Block off that vacation time. Call your family even when you're exhausted. And for the love of all things holy, stop saying yes to every last-minute trip. Your career will thank you. And most importantly, your family will thank you. "The most important work you will ever do will be within the walls of your own home." ~ Harold B. Lee

CHAPTER 7

Financial Planning
for Contract Pilots

Budgeting for a Variable Income

One of the greatest joys of contract flying is that your paycheck can be wildly different from one month to the next. One month, you're raking in cash like a hedge fund manager. The next month, you're staring at your bank account, trying to determine if you have enough money to splurge on the premium gas station coffee or if you should stick with the free, highly questionable FBO brew. Managing a fluctuating income is a challenge, and if you don't get a handle on it early, you'll end up broke and wondering if you should've just stayed at your last job.

How to Handle Fluctuating Paychecks

A common mistake newer contract pilots make is acting like every good month is going to last forever. It's easy to fall into the trap of looking at a fat paycheck or strong month and immediately deciding that you "deserve" a new watch, a fancy dinner, or, god forbid, a boat. Bad idea. The reality is that contract flying is seasonal, unpredictable, and sometimes cruel. If you don't plan ahead, you'll be the guy who made bank in December and then spent January wondering if you can pay your mortgage.

The way to survive the financial rollercoaster of contract flying is to budget based on your worst months, not your best ones. If your highest-earning month was $25,000, but your slowest month was $6,000, you need to budget like you're making $6,000 every month. Anything above that goes straight into savings (not a new watch, not a third iPad, and definitely not an ill-advised impulse purchase like a vintage motorcycle that will sit in your garage). This isn't pessimism; it's financial survivalism. Your future self will thank you when slow times come.

Building a Financial Safety Net

Whether you call it a "financial safety net" or an "emergency fund," you're going to need one. It's like having extra runway length. Every contract pilot will experience unexpected slow periods, delayed payments, or a last-minute cancellation that wipes out half their income for the month. If you don't have a cushion, you'll be one bad month away from panic.

The smartest contractors keep at least three to six months' worth of expenses saved up. That way, when the inevitable dry spell hits, they aren't frantically taking terrible jobs just to keep the lights on. I made this mistake once when a client's payment was "delayed" (translation: he conveniently forgot I existed for six weeks). At first, I told myself, "No big deal, I'll just wait it out." But after a couple of weeks, I was reaching out to the client so that I could make ends meet. Lesson learned: always have a backup fund.

This safety net also gives you bargaining power. If you're not desperate for cash, you can turn down bad or low-paying trips. Operators love pilots who will fly for peanuts, but they won't respect you for it. Having savings allows you to say no when necessary, ensuring you hold out for the jobs that actually pay what you're worth.

Planning for Unexpected Expenses

Just like we discussed earlier in Chapter 5 about planning for contingencies during flight ops, the same is true when planning for unexpected financial expenses. In the event of a sudden car repair, an unexpected tax bill, or a medical expense, you need to be ready. There is no paycheck fairy who magically bails out contract pilots when things go sideways.

One fine April morning, I woke up feeling particularly smug about my financial situation. My bank account looked solid, my flights were booked for the next month, and I even considered treating myself to some personal time off in the near future. Then, that very afternoon, my accountant called with some pretty depressing news. By her calculations, my tax liability was much larger than she had quoted me throughout the year. Of course, when I queried her on this large miscalculation, she replied, "Hey, look on the bright side—you made more money this year!" Cue the emergency fund.

The choice is yours as to how much is enough. Whatever you decide, having a financial cushion for the inevitable is the difference between handling an emergency with mild irritation and handling it with full-scale financial setback.

If you're used to a W-2 flying job where taxes are magically stolen—I mean deducted—from your paycheck before you ever see a dime, welcome to the Wild West of self-employment taxation. If you're not setting aside money for taxes every time you get paid, you're going to have a rude awakening come tax season. The IRS does not take "I forgot" as a valid excuse, and they have far less patience for financial mismanagement than your local FBO does when you forget to pay for fuel. A good rule of thumb? Set aside at least 25 to 30 percent of every paycheck for taxes. Yes, it hurts. But it hurts a lot less than realizing in April that you owe the IRS more money than you have in your bank account. Trust me on this one.

Taxes, Deductions, and Retirement Planning

Speaking of taxes, no matter how many cool jets you fly or the exotic destinations you fly to, I can assure you the taxman will cometh. Contract pilots are not just skilled aviators; we're also the CFO and chief accountant of You, Inc. This means you need to be just as comfortable navigating the IRS tax code as you are navigating an ILS approach to minimums.

Maximizing Tax Deductions as a Freelancer

When you first start out in contract flying, you may not be making a whole lot of money initially. This can lull you into complacency when things get busier and your income increases. Make sure you are not making the classic mistake of assuming taxes would "work themselves out" like they did when you were a W-2 pilot/earner. That fantasy can turn into a nightmare when the IRS expects you to cough up a hefty chunk of your earnings.

The good news? The tax code, while soul-crushingly complex, does offer some relief for the savvy independent contractor.

Deductions are your best friend. You can write off a shocking number of work-related expenses, provided you keep meticulous records and don't try to claim your dog as an emotional support business asset. Need a new flight bag? Deductible. Need a new headset because yours mysteriously stopped working? Deductible. Training costs, type ratings, fuel expenses, per diems, and even a portion of your home office (if you use it strictly for work) are all deductible. But here's the trick: you have to document everything. The IRS doesn't operate on an honor system, and a tax audit is about as fun as a holding pattern over Chicago in a thunderstorm. Keep your receipts, track mileage for work-related travel, and don't round up your expenses to the nearest thousand unless you want a friendly letter from the IRS. Spend some time continuing to learn about other tax-saving strategies that may work for you on places like Pro Pilot World, PPRuNe, and pro-pilot podcasts like 21.Five because the laws are constantly changing.

Setting Up Retirement Accounts (IRA, 401(k), etc.)

If you've spent any time as a contract pilot, you've probably met some old-timers who have no plans to retire—ever. Not because they love flying that much, but because they never set up a retirement plan and now have no choice but to keep going until their knees give out. Don't be that guy.

Unlike airline pilots, who have/had pensions, employer-matched 401(k)s, and union-backed retirement planning at their fingertips, contract pilots have whatever they set up for themselves. That means if you don't take retirement planning seriously, you'll be flying well past the age where your bifocals can keep up with the glass cockpit.

The good news? Freelancers have decent retirement options—if they take advantage of them. You are somewhat forced into the investments the IRS allows to mitigate your tax liability. Individual Retirement Accounts (IRAs) and Solo 401(k)s let you stash away pre-tax dollars so that Future You isn't shaking his fist at Present You for spending everything on high-end sunglasses and unnecessary pilot gadgets.

Here's a breakdown of the most common retirement fund options for the self-employed:

- **Traditional IRA:** Contribute up to $7,000 per year ($8,000 if you're over fifty), and your contributions are tax-deductible. You'll pay taxes when you withdraw it in retirement, but you get the benefit of tax-deferred growth.

- **Roth IRA:** You pay taxes on contributions now, but when you retire, your withdrawals are tax-free. This is great if you think tax rates will go up. Limits are the same as the Traditional IRA

- **Solo 401(k):** You can contribute both as an employee AND an employer, which means in 2024, you can sock away up to $66,000 if you structure it right.

- **Health Savings Account (HAS):** Up to $8,300 for a family and $4,150 for singles (2025)

- **SEP IRA:** Can contribute 25 percent of net earnings up to $70,000 (2025)

- **Self-Directed IRA:** Invest beyond typical stocks and bonds

My first year of contract flying, I ignored retirement planning entirely because I was too busy getting my business off the ground to think about Future Me. But by year two, I set up some accounts and started getting serious about my contributions. I realized retirement wasn't just a distant concept but something I could actively plan for that would help mitigate tax liability. Start with some sort of suitable plan, contribute often, and don't underestimate the power of compounding.

Health Insurance and Benefits for Independent Contractors

If you've ever wondered why airline pilots cling so tightly to their jobs despite the bureaucratic nightmares and years-long upgrade lists, I have two words for you: health insurance. For the self-employed, health insurance is the financial equivalent of an emergency landing at night in a storm with only one working engine—terrifying, complicated, and requiring careful navigation. Unlike our airline brethren, who have HR departments spoon-feeding them benefits, us contractors have to figure it out ourselves.

Here are a few survival strategies:

1. **Join a Professional Association:** Groups like NBAA and AOPA offer health insurance plans for members. It won't always be cheaper, but it's a solid option.

2. **High-Deductible Plans with HSAs:** These are great for healthy pilots who just need coverage for catastrophic events. An HSA (Health Savings Account) lets you save pre-tax money for medical expenses, which is the closest thing to a tax break you'll get on healthcare. I really like the triple tax advantage here too.

3. **Shop Around:** The Affordable Care Act (ACA) marketplace offers plans, but costs vary. Some states have better deals than others.

4. **Use a Spouse's Policy:** A spouse may be able to add you to their policy for a reasonable rate.

The trick with health insurance is finding something you can afford that still covers you when you actually need it. If you go cheap and just pray you don't get sick, you're rolling the dice on your financial stability. In the U.S., a good old-fashioned hospital visit can be more expensive than a lap through the judicial system. It's like adding insult to injury when you get the bill. Do like the Scouts, and "Be Prepared" here.

Investing in Your Career for Long-Term Success

Flying airplanes for a living is great, but you need a long-term plan. Contract flying can be a lucrative career, but it can also be as unpredictable as a summer thunderstorm in Florida. Surviving and thriving means investing in your career. Not just in terms of money, but also in time, strategy, and forward thinking. A smart contractor doesn't just bank on today's paycheck; they're always planning for tomorrow's opportunities. If you're not actively working to expand your income, optimize your financial strategy, and set yourself up for future success, you'll wake up one day wondering where the last twenty years went and why you still can't afford that retirement house in Florida.

Finding Additional Streams of Income

One myth of contract flying is that pilots only make money flying airplanes. That's only true if you lack imagination. Any experienced aviation career coach will tell you that the most successful pilots aren't just the ones logging the most hours; they're the ones diversifying their income streams.

Some pilots tap into additional income by writing aviation articles, consulting for aircraft owners, ferry flying, instructing, or even flipping airplanes. I know a guy who spent his downtime scouring aircraft sales listings, buying undervalued planes, doing a bit of work on them, and flipping them for profit. It was essentially House Hunters: Aviation Edition, but without the annoying real estate agents. The point is, if you're only making money when you're flying, you're limiting yourself. There are countless ways to turn your aviation expertise into additional income; you just have to get creative.

Financial Strategies to Stay Ahead

Flying for a living is one thing; flying for a comfortable retirement is another. Most pilots are great at planning flight routes but terrible at planning their financial future. It's not enough to make money— you need to know how to manage it.

One of the best pieces of financial advice I ever got came from someone outside the industry. They told me, "If you live like you make half of what you actually earn, you'll never worry about money." And it's true. Too many contract pilots fall into the feast-or-famine cycle. They spend like royalty when the jobs are rolling in, then scramble like a broke college student when things slow down. The trick is to treat every paycheck as if the slow months are already here.

A solid financial strategy starts with saving aggressively and investing wisely. Retirement accounts are great (we covered those in the last section), but you should also look at investments outside of aviation. Real estate, index funds, and even side businesses that generate passive income. They can all keep you financially stable when flying work slows down.

One of the biggest mistakes I see contract pilots make is spending too much money on things that don't make them more money. You don't need a brand-new Rolex, a new car every two years, or some other high-priced widget you've been fantasizing about. You do need training, additional type ratings, and networking opportunities that will keep your career moving forward and your income growing.

If you have extra cash, don't blow it on fancy toys; invest it in yourself. Attend the NBAA conference where the big-shot hiring managers are hanging out. Upgrade your résumé and LinkedIn profile so you actually stand out. Spend a little on marketing or website design. The best financial strategy is one that keeps your career growing, not just your collection of expensive watches.

Planning for Future Career Moves

No contract pilot should ever assume they'll be doing the same thing forever. Aviation is an industry of constant change, and if you don't evolve with it, you'll be left behind. Planning for your future career moves doesn't mean you need to have everything mapped out to the minute, but you do need to have a general sense of where you want to be in five, ten, and twenty years.

I've met contract pilots who swore they'd never take a full-time job, only to realize ten years later that they were sick of the uncertainty and wanted a more stable gig. I've also met full-time corporate pilots who, after years of company politics and rigid schedules, made the leap to contract flying and never looked back.

If you're a contract pilot now, ask yourself: What does life look like in five years? Where do you want to be in your career? Do you want to move up to larger jets? Fly internationally? Transition into an aircraft management role? Teach? Have more time off? The best contract pilots aren't just reacting to career shifts; they're actively shaping what they want their future to look like.

Conclusion

Budgeting as a contract pilot is not for the weak. Your income is unpredictable, and every once in a while, life throws you an expensive curveball at you. But if you plan smartly, you can avoid the feast-or-famine cycles that trap so many freelancers.

The key to financial success as a contract pilot is budgeting based on your lowest-earning months, not your highest. When you have a great month, save it. Build a financial safety net that lets you survive slow periods without panic and gives you the freedom to turn down bad offers.

Take charge of your taxes, retirement, and health insurance. Maximize your deductions, but keep records. Set up a retirement plan early because Social Security alone won't cut it (and might not even be around by the time you retire). And for the love of all things good, get health insurance before you need it. Being a contract pilot can mean freedom, flexibility, and the ability to make great money, but only if you plan wisely. So take care of Future You.

Investing in your career isn't just about money; it's about developing a long-term strategy that ensures you're always in demand, financially stable, and in control of your future. Find multiple streams of income to keep your finances strong. Plan for future career moves and stay in tune with industry trends.

At the end of the day, a career in contract flying is what you make of it. If you treat it like a short-term hustle, that's all it will ever be. But if you invest in yourself, plan ahead, and make smart financial decisions, you can build a career that's profitable, sustainable, and—most importantly—one that keeps you flying on your own terms. After all, isn't that the whole point of doing this in the first place?

CHAPTER 8

Long-Term Success & Expanding Your Opportunities

Scaling Your Contract Pilot Business

The thing about contract flying is that once you get a taste for the freedom, it's hard to go back. The idea of a set schedule, wearing a company uniform, and listening to a chief pilot drone about crew rest and duty limits in a meeting that could have been an email? No, thank you. But as great as freelancing is, making it sustainable for the long haul requires strategy, smart decisions, and a little bit of creativity. It's not enough to just book trips and hope for the best.—You have to scale your business so that you're not constantly chasing the next gig. The goal is to turn contract flying from a job into a fully-fledged business that works for you, not the other way around.

How to Go from Part-Time to Full-Time Freelancing

There are two kinds of pilots who dabble in contract flying. First, there are those who test the waters while still holding onto their full-time job. They pick up an occasional freelance trip here and there to see if they like it, all while keeping that sweet company-paid health insurance and other benefits. Then, there are those who have jumped headfirst into full-time freelancing, realizing they can make more money in half the hours while avoiding corporate nonsense.

So, how do you make the leap successfully? By planning ahead and not just assuming the work will magically appear.

When I first started taking on contract gigs, I figured I could simply tell a few people I was available, and the jobs would come rolling in. This was incredibly incorrect. The first month, I had exactly two trips, which barely covered my rent and made me consider whether or not I should pick up a side hustle delivering food at the airport. When I started treating contract flying as a real business, things turned around. That meant constantly working on my schedule, reaching out to operators proactively, and making sure I wasn't just waiting for work. I had to go out and find it.

Hopefully, by now, I have stressed the importance of building a strong network. And that is exactly what you want to do before making the jump. If you're thinking of going full-time as a contract pilot, start booking gigs while you have your regular job. Test out different operators, see who pays on time (and who mysteriously "forgets"), and get a feel for what a sustainable workload looks like. When your contract flying income starts outpacing your full-time salary, you know it's time to make the leap. And when you do, have at least three to six months of expenses saved up because contract flying, like all freelancing, has its slow months. You want to have the boat as close to the dock as possible before making the jump.

Adding Additional Aviation-Related Income Streams

As a contract pilot, understand that you cannot rely solely on flying gigs to pay the bills. The industry is unpredictable. One minute, you're turning down jobs because you're too busy, and the next, you're sitting at home wondering why your phone isn't ringing. The solution is to diversify your income.

One pilot I know started coordinating charter trips for clients and turned this into a nice additional revenue stream. Another pilot I know works as a consultant for aircraft owners, advising them on hiring pilots, managing maintenance schedules, and understanding operational costs. He still flies, but now he also gets paid to talk about flying. Aviation career coaches often suggest that pilots look for ways to monetize their expertise beyond just flying. That could mean:

- Teaching ground school courses
- Selling checklists and training guides
- Developing an aviation-related YouTube channel (because, apparently, people love watching pilots talk about airplanes)

The key is to find something that complements your flying career without taking up all of your time. The best side income streams are the ones that work in the background, bringing in money while you're still out there flying.

Coaching, Consulting, and Mentoring Other Pilots

One of the shifts that happens when you start establishing yourself in contract flying is that other pilots start asking you for advice. At first, it's just a friend or two asking, "Hey, how did you get started?" Then, before you know it, you're getting emails from strangers saying, "I heard you're the guy to talk to about contract flying." This is where new income streams start to take shape.

Mentorship is one of the more valuable things a seasoned contract pilot can offer. It helps the next generation of pilots and can be a side business if done correctly. Pilots will pay good money for personalized coaching that helps them set up their freelance business, understand contracts, and navigate the world of aviation networking.

Offer a one-hour coaching call to new freelancers. You may ask, "Who would pay for that?" Turns out, a lot of people. Sharing the knowledge you have already gained through experience can shave a lot of time off and save a lot of heartache for the 'up-and-comers.' If you have years of experience and know the ins and outs of the business, there's absolutely no reason you shouldn't be leveraging that knowledge. Whether it's formal coaching, consulting, or just creating digital resources for new pilots, there are endless ways to turn what you already know into another revenue stream.

Adapting to Industry Changes

The only thing predictable about corporate aviation is that it's completely unpredictable. One day, you're comfortably riding the wave of high demand, and the next, you're staring at job boards, wondering if you should dust off that résumé. The pilots who thrive are the best at adapting. If you want long-term success, you have to keep an eye on how things are changing, stay ahead of industry trends, and figure out how to remain relevant in a job market that can turn on a dime.

How Technology Is Shaping Corporate Aviation

There was a time when being a corporate pilot meant you had to be half-aviator and half-magician, flying on gut instinct with paper charts and the occasional lucky guess. Now, with the speed at which aviation technology is evolving, it sometimes feels like these aircraft are an endless supply of information. The screens are sleek, the data is instantaneous, and the aircraft is practically whispering, "I got this, buddy."

With advancements like autonomous flight technology, AI-driven predictive maintenance, and real-time data streaming, corporate pilots have to keep up or get left behind. The truth is that corporate aviation is moving toward more automation, more efficiency, and fewer pilots who refuse to learn new systems. If you want to stay competitive, you better embrace the tech.

Staying proficient in the latest avionics and flight management systems isn't optional; it's a survival skill. New aircraft are being designed with technology that reduces pilot workload. Learning how to work with these systems will keep you in demand long after the old-school pilots have aged out of the job market.

Trends in Private Jet Demand and Pilot Hiring

No matter what happens in the economy, there will always be people who don't want to be herded through a large airport like cattle, only to sit next to some guy sneezing on a commercial flight. That's where we come in.

The demand for private jets skyrocketed after the pandemic, as people realized they could avoid the horrors of TSA, middle seats, and delayed flights by simply throwing money at the problem. Private jet charters, fractional ownership programs, and corporate flight departments have all seen an increase in demand. And guess what? They need pilots.

Operators are now looking for pilots who are more than just stick-and-rudder experts. They want pilots who can provide exceptional customer service, adapt to constantly changing schedules, and understand the business side of private aviation. Yes, there is a priority on experience, training, and type ratings, but now soft skills matter. Pilots who can adapt to clients' needs and stay professional under pressure will land the better gigs.

Staying Competitive in an Evolving Job Market

The contract pilots who adapt to industry changes and market trends keep working while everyone else scrambles to catch up. The job market in corporate aviation is constantly shifting, and what worked five years ago might not work today.

The pilots who stay ahead are the ones who are constantly updating their skills, expanding their networks, and paying attention to where the industry is headed. They're the ones who attend aviation conferences, keep up with emerging technologies, and make sure they're always ready for the next opportunity.

If you're looking to stay competitive, invest in yourself. Determine the type of training that is in demand in your market and go after it. Set goals to attend networking events, get involved with pilot organizations, and continually market yourself, even when you don't think you need to. The aviation career coaches will tell you the same thing: the best jobs don't go to the best pilots; they go to the best-connected, best-prepared pilots.

Mapping Out Your Future in Aviation

There comes a point in every pilot's career when they stop asking, "Where's my next trip?" and start asking, "Where's my career actually going?" For some, the goal is simple: fly until they pry your hands off the yoke. For others, it's about figuring out how to make all those years of experience pay off in a way that doesn't involve living out of a suitcase forever. Long-term success in corporate aviation isn't just flying; it's figuring out what comes next before next sneaks up on you and slaps you with a dose of reality.

Long-Term Career Goals and Exit Strategies

If you've been flying long enough, you've probably seen two types of pilots: those who planned for their future and those who just kept flying until, one day, someone told them they couldn't anymore. You don't want to be in the second group.

When I first started flying, I had this vague idea that I'd fly forever. Retirement? Exit strategy? Those were things for airline pilots with pensions and stock options, not contractors who spent half their lives chasing the next trip. But one day, I had a conversation with a mentor who said, "You know, at some point, you're gonna want to land for good. Might as well have a plan for it."

The idea of an exit strategy doesn't have to mean quitting aviation. It just means having a plan for what comes next. Some pilots transition into flight department management, others shift into aircraft sales, and some pursue a full-time career in training and mentoring younger pilots. Start thinking about it before your body (or the industry) makes the decision for you.

Transitioning into Aircraft Management or Ownership

For contract pilots, the idea of managing an aircraft can seem about as appealing as voluntarily sitting through an FAA seminar on airspace improvement. But if you do it right, aircraft management can be your golden parachute.

A lot of pilots find themselves managing aircraft simply because they became the "go-to" guy for an owner who trusted them. One day, you're just flying the jet; the next, the owner is asking if you can "handle a few things," like scheduling maintenance, hiring crew, and making sure the aircraft doesn't turn into an expensive paperweight. Before you know it, you're not just a pilot—you're a full-blown aircraft manager.

The transition into aircraft management can be a natural step for contract pilots who want more stability without giving up the aviation lifestyle. It means less hopping from gig to gig and more building long-term relationships with owners and operators. It also means more responsibility, but it can provide a steady paycheck and a sense of control over your career that solely doing contract work lacks.

Some pilots partner with investors to buy and lease aircraft. They might start with smaller planes, such as King Airs or Citations, and build up from there. There are pilots who turn this aircraft ownership into a business, using fractional ownership models or leasing their planes out for charter. Understanding the numbers and legalities is key here. But it's a good way to transition away from just flying to earn and into more of an asset-earning based business within aviation.

Building a Legacy in Corporate Aviation

Most pilots don't think about their "legacy" in their aviation careers. But leaving a mark on corporate aviation as a contractor can have an impact that lasts beyond your final landing. Some pilots build their legacy by mentoring the next generation. They take younger pilots under their wing, teaching them not just how to fly but how to survive in the business. Others leave a mark by starting their own flight departments, building businesses, or pioneering new approaches to corporate aviation.

Once you have built up a solid client base, you can launch an aviation consulting company. Now, instead of chasing trips, you can help aircraft owners navigate everything from purchases to operations and get paid handsomely for it. Your legacy in corporate aviation doesn't have to be a grand, sweeping enterprise. It can be as simple as being the guy (or gal) who took the time to help others, built a strong reputation, and left the industry a little better than they found it.

Conclusion

Scaling your contract pilot business isn't about working harder; it's about working smarter. The pilots who make the most money and have the best careers are the ones who build multiple revenue streams, plan ahead, and invest in their long-term success.

If you're transitioning from part-time to full-time freelancing, treat it like a business, not just a side gig. Build a strong network, create a financial buffer, and don't just wait for opportunities. Go out and make them happen.

Adding additional income streams ensures that you're never at the mercy of the contract-flying market. Write, teach, sell, consult—do something that brings in revenue even when you're not in the cockpit. And when you've built enough experience, help other pilots do the same. Whether it's coaching, consulting, or mentoring, your knowledge has value, so use it.

Corporate aviation isn't going anywhere, but it is changing. If you want long-term success, you have to adapt to new technology, understand hiring trends, and stay ahead in a competitive job market.

Technology is making aircraft smarter. Make sure you're smart enough to keep up. Private jet demand is evolving. Make sure you evolve with it. If you want to fly long-term, stay sharp, stay adaptable, and never stop learning.

Flying corporate jets is great, but flying with a plan for your future is even better. Whether it's transitioning into aircraft management, ownership, or continuing to build your aviation business, there are plenty of ways to keep growing in this industry. And when it comes to building a legacy, the best pilots are remembered for their impact.

Your Next Steps to Becoming a Successful Contract Pilot

Taking Action Today

So here you are, ready to spread your wings and take flight as a contract pilot. Whether you're fresh off your ATP check ride or transitioning from a long airline career, the contract flying world is full of opportunity, challenges, and freedom. It won't always be easy, and you'll face slow months, late-night calls, last-minute changes, and clients with very specific requests that may seem outlandish. But if you treat this like the business it is, you're building a lifestyle that puts you in control of your time, your earnings, and your future.

Start today. Polish up that résumé, reach out to operators and managers, and get your name out there. Pick one step from this book and take action—whether it's building your website, joining a professional network, or simply connecting with a mentor who's already in the game. Build your brand, get your paperwork in order, and start saying yes to opportunities (even the ones that scare you a little).

Below is a quick start checklist for you to begin your journey as a contract pilot. Also, there are some resources where flying opportunities get posted daily. Don't be afraid to use mentorship programs, coaching services, and the experiences of those who've gone before you to shortcut the learning curve. Contract flying is a calling for those who value independence, variety, and professional growth. The sky is wide open.

Quick-Start Checklist to Launch Your Contract Pilot Career

If you're ready to get serious about contract flying, here's your quick-start checklist to go from dreaming about it to actually doing it:

1. Get Your Qualifications in Order
   - ☐ Ensure you meet minimum flight hour requirements for the aircraft you want to fly.
   - ☐ Obtain necessary type ratings (a focus on high-demand jets can open more doors).
   - ☐ Keep your credentials current, including medical certificate, type ratings, and IPC/Flight review.

2. Set Up Your Business
   - ☐ Decide between an LLC or sole proprietorship.
   - ☐ Get the proper insurance.
   - ☐ Open a dedicated business bank account.

3. Build Your Personal Brand
   - ☐ Update (or create) a professional aviation résumé highlighting your experience.
   - ☐ Establish an online presence.
   - ☐ Present yourself as a top-tier contract pilot.

4. Start Networking and Marketing Yourself

- ☐ Attend NBAA events, aviation expos, and pilot meetups to make industry connections.
- ☐ Reach out to flight departments, operators, and staffing agencies.
- ☐ Join pilot networks, Facebook groups, and forums where jobs are frequently posted.

5. Land Your First Contract Gigs

- ☐ Be willing to take short-term or last-minute jobs to get your foot in the door.
- ☐ Always exceed expectations.
- ☐ Build a reliable reputation.

6. Manage Your Finances Wisely

- ☐ Budget for variable income.
- ☐ Track all deductible expenses (travel, training, equipment, etc.).
- ☐ Set aside at least 30 percent of your income for taxes.

Resources for Training, Networking, and Job Searching

Training and Type Ratings:

- • FlightSafety International
- • CAE
- • LOFT flight training
- • Executive Flight Training

Job Boards:

- • Climbto350.com

- BizJetJobs.com
- Find A Pilot.com
- NBAA Jobs Board
- In-Flight Crew Connections
- Flight Crews Unlimited
- Flight Crew International
- Local aircraft managers
- Local aircraft owners

Networking and Industry Groups:

- National Business Aviation Association (NBAA)
- Pro Pilot World
- LinkedIn
- Facebook groups like "CAJL Contract Pilots Network," "Contract Pilots," and "Corporate Aviation Job Listings"
- PPRuNe
- CJP
- Business aviation forums
- Local FBO's

About the Author

Joshua Vinson is a veteran contract pilot and aviation consultant with over twenty years of experience flying corporate jets across North America. Based in the St. Louis area, he founded Mid America Aviation to provide professional pilot services, mentor pilots, and promote contract flying as a flexible, high-reward career path. Learn more at http://www.midamerica-aviation.com.

www.ingramcontent.com/pod-product-compliance
Lightning Source LLC
Chambersburg PA
CBHW070456130626
46555CB00003B/1030